EXPLORING
WICCA

EXPLORING WICCA

WICCA

The Beliefs, Rites, and Rituals of the
Wiccan Religion

By
Lady Sabrina

NEW PAGE BOOKS
A division of The Career Press, Inc.
Franklin Lakes, NJ

Copyright © 2001 by Lady Sabrina

EXPLORING WICCA
Cover design by Lu Rossman
Printed in the U.S.A. by Book-mart Press

To order this title, please call toll-free 1-800-CAREER-1 (NJ and Canada: 201-848-0310) to order using VISA or Master Card, or for further information on books from Career Press.

The Career Press, Inc., 3 Tice Road, PO Box 687,
Franklin Lakes, NJ 07417
www.careerpress.com
www.newpagebooks.com

Library of Congress Cataloging-in-Publication Data

Sabrina, Lady.
    Exploring Wicca : the beliefs, rites, and rituals of the Wiccan religion /
by Lady Sabrina.
       p.   cm.
    Includes bibliographical references and index.
    ISBN 1-56414-481-X (pbk.)
    1. Witchcraft. I. Title.

BF1566 .S23 2000
299—dc21
                                     00-035516

Dedication

This book is dedicated to the solitary practitioner of Wicca and the magickal arts, and to the students and members of Our Lady of Enchantment, especially Aristaeus and Autumn, who provided endless help and technical support.

Most of all, special thanks go to Mike Lewis, who is responsible for making this book a reality. Thank you, Mike!

Contents

Introduction   9

1. The Wiccan Religion   13

2. Principles of Wiccan Belief   21

3. Wiccan Roots: The Celtic Druids   31

4. Deity: The God and Goddess   41

5. Wiccan Myth and Scripture   57

6. The Four Elements   67

7. Sacred Wiccan Symbols   77

8. The Wiccan Temple   83

9. Fundamental Rites   91

10. Seasons of Celebration   115

11. Wicca and Magick   153

12. Spellcrafting and Natural Magick   165

13. Resources for Exploring Wicca   183

Glossary   195

Recommended Reading   205

Bibliography   211

Index   215

About the Author   221

Introduction

Witchcraft, also called Wicca, or simply the Craft, is considered to be the Old Religion, because it is based on the religious practices of our Pagan ancestors. As a religion, Wicca celebrates life, is earth and fertility oriented, and worships the divine as personified in the form of a Goddess and a God. Moreover, the Craft encourages the use of psychic power and magick to bring physical desire into fruition.

The main reason Witchcraft has survived through the millennia is because its philosophy has always been fluid—

able to adapt, change, and contribute to the social structure of its time. Additionally, Wicca has always encouraged its adherents to do things according to the natural order and to see the connectedness of all life. This embracing of nature and her ways tends to develop strength of will and character within the devotee.

One outstanding feature of the Wiccan religion is the status it accords its adherents. Women and men are both respected members of the priesthood; groups (covens) meet and worship within a circle where all are considered equal; and individuals are encouraged to develop their own spiritual ideals and style of worship.

Wicca is an all-embracing spiritual philosophy and way of life to its followers. In its simplest form, the practice of Witchcraft is a process of learning to understand nature and tread her paths with confidence and pride. In its most complex form, Wicca facilitates the creation process and permits the individual to manifest desire, in accordance with his or her own will. Simply put, Wicca helps people reclaim their personal power and spiritual individuality.

The Wiccan religion is unique in that it lacks the hierarchical doctrine imposed by most organized religions. There is no Pope or spiritual elder to dictate morals or impose punishment. There are no specific doctrines one must follow, other than the good sense offered by the Wiccan Rede: "An it harm none, do what ye will."

Wicca is considered to be an oral tradition, which means it is passed from one individual to another by the spoken word. In general, it is taught in small groups known as covens. Spiritual knowledge is gained through extensive reading, as well as through personal experience. It is through personal experience that individuals learn how to live in harmony with their surroundings as they grow and progress spiritually.

This book is geared toward the seeker and solitary practitioner who wants to learn how to practice Wicca but is unsure of where to begin. The book does not follow or support any specific Wiccan tradition or path, rather it concentrates on those beliefs most Wiccans hold in common. Therefore, this book is a good place to start for those curious about Wicca or in training for its priesthood.

I suggest that you take your time and learn to appreciate the subtle nuances upon which the Craft is based. By doing this, you will gain the necessary knowledge and understanding you need to truly take advantage of all the Craft has to offer. Wicca is more than just a once a week trip to church — it is a way of life.

Chapter 1

The Wiccan Religion

*"Religion. A daughter of hope and fear, explaining
to ignorance the nature of the unknowable."*
—Ambrose Bierce

To thousands of practitioners, Witchcraft is more
than just a religion; it is a way of life, involving a
complex mixture of magic, ritual custom, and reverence for deity. In its principal modern form, Wicca traces its
origins back to the early 1940s and a British occultist named

Gerald Gardner. It was Gardner's frustration with both Christianity and Ceremonial Magic (which uses psychic skills through rituals, traditions, and the laws of nature), the only "occult" alternative, that prompted him to create something different.

Gerald Gardner's religion was based on pre-existing spiritual concepts, which he combined in a new way to form a new system. His mixing of ceremonial magic with hereditary Witchcraft and Masonic ritual was nothing less than genius. And, with the help of people like Doreen Valiente, Dion Fortune, Ross Nichols, and other notable scholars, he was able to create a new and dynamic religion.

Witchcraft, or Wicca, as we know it today, is not the sole survivor of antiquity, nor is it an entirely modern creation. Rather, it is a blend of many different spiritual persuasions. Despite the fact that Pagan rites, Shamanic customs, and Goddess worship predate Christianity, there is still no reliable evidence of an established Wiccan religion before 1951.

After the final repeal of the English Witchcraft Act in 1951, Gerald Gardner broke the vow of secrecy he held with the New Forest Coven. He published several books and soon the whole world knew that Witchcraft was alive and well and being openly practiced.

From the early 1960s and on, people involved with Witchcraft, magick, and related Pagan ideals began to speak out. More books appeared on the market, covens were started, and Wicca was on its way to becoming a recognizable religion. Today, there are hundreds of Wiccan organizations in the United States and Europe that support Gerald Gardner's ideas.

One reason that Witchcraft has become so popular is that it tends to focus on the individual. Wiccans are taught to think for themselves, take responsibility for their lives, and live by the Wiccan Rede, a sort of a witches' golden rule, which says, "An ye harm none, do what ye will."

Most Wiccans are attracted to the Craft because it helps them regain their personal power and rekindles their spiritual desire. In some cases, the lure is the Goddess herself. The idea of balance between sexes, rather than male superiority, and the feminine leadership in the Wiccan priesthood are very attractive to many Wiccans.

Modern Witchcraft has two branches, Devotional and Functional. Devotional Witchcraft deals primarily with the worship of the God and Goddess, whereas Functional Witchcraft employs the use of magic in its rites. Both classes work with the phases of the moon and the changing of the seasons to enhance mystical rites.

Within the Wiccan movement, there are various subgroups, known as Traditions. Traditions are Wiccan spiritual systems built from an individual or group's emotional and learned experiences that are repeated and shared over a number of years, eventually creating an organized belief and ritual practice. Most of the well-known Traditions that have managed to survive are descendants of original or hereditary sources. Others are the modern creations of scholars and notable authors.

Gardnerian Wicca

Gerald Gardner set the precedent for the modern Wiccan movement. Sometime during the late 1930s, Gardner was introduced to a hereditary Witch named Old Dorothy Cluterbuck, who initiated him into a group called the New Forest Coven. Prior to this, Gardner had been involved with the Masons, Oriental mysticism, and the Golden Dawn system of ceremonial magic. Gardner's new religion did not blossom overnight. It took years to perfect, with the input of other Witches and occultists. Gardner's publication of three books, *High Magick's Aid* (1949), *Witchcraft Today* (1954), and *The Meaning of Witchcraft* (1959), brought the Wiccan ideal out into the open.

The religion that Gardner created, Gardnerian Wicca, stresses the worship of the Goddess and the Horned God. Covens are always headed by a High Priestess, and they have three degrees of initiation, paralleling those of the Masons. Religious celebrations occur at the eight seasonal shifts, and full moons are considered to be a time of great power and potential.

Most Gardnerian groups work skyclad (naked), and polarity (the balance between the masculine and feminine) is emphasized. Covens tend to have equal numbers of male and female initiates, and couples are encouraged to join. During ritual, power is raised through chanting, meditation, and symbolic sexual union, as enacted during the Great Rite. Symbolic tools include the four weapons of ceremonial magic (wand, athame, chalice, and pentacle), in addition to the scourge and cord.

Alexandrian Wicca

Alexandrian Wicca, an offshoot of Gardnerian Wicca, was founded in the early 1960s by Alex Sanders and his wife, Maxine. Alex Sanders proclaimed himself "King of the Witches"; he claimed to have been initiated at age 7 by his grandmother. This was later found to be untrue, as it was revealed he had been initiated into a regular Gardnerian coven.

Alexandrian Wicca tends to focus on training, and it places much more emphasis on ceremonial magic, than most Gardnerian groups do. Alexandrian Wiccans make use of Kabbalah, the magical system of the ancient Hebrews, and Enochian, the magical language of angels, which has its own alphabet and grammar. Covens usually meet once a week for training, and at full moons and seasonal shifts for worship. Most Alexandrian Witches work skyclad, use the same symbolic tools as Gardnerians, and stress initiation as the formal means of entrance into the group.

Dianic Wicca

There are two distinct branches of Dianic Wicca. The first is Old Dianic, formed in the early 1960s by Morgan McFarland and Mark Roberts. This original branch of Dianic Wicca places primary importance upon the Goddess, but still recognizes and honors the Horned God as her consort. Emphasis is on reclaiming female power and the goddess within. Rituals are eclectic. Tools and times of celebration are the same as Gardnerian Wicca.

The second branch of Dianic Witchcraft is feminist in orientation. Only women are allowed, and only the Goddess is worshiped. Often covens have lesbian participants only. Most groups are loosely structured, rituals are often experimental and spontaneous, and symbolism will vary from one group to another. The focus is always on the female aspect, and there is usually a political agenda attached to the group.

Eclectic Wicca

This branch of Wicca covers groups and individuals who do not follow any one tradition, but who rather incorporate the elements of several different traditions into their practices. They work with different deities from different pantheons, rather than concentrating on one specific god and goddess. Eclectic Wiccans mix and match symbols, myths, and ceremonies according to preference and experience.

Hereditary/Traditional Wicca

Witchcraft practiced within a family unit that lays claim to a lineage predating the Gardnerian revival is considered Hereditary or Traditional. In the early days of Wicca (1960s and 70s) this was the bandwagon to be on. Many, many people claimed a Wiccan heritage that extended from the dawn of time and was passed down to them by their grandmothers. It seems that in the 1960s and 70s grandmothers were a busy lot, baking, sewing, and initiating the wee ones into Witchcraft!

Generally, the Hereditary Witch comes from a family that practiced folk magic and herbal medicine. In the case of a true Hereditary Witch, there will be cogent evidence of the direct line of descent from ancestors who were initiated Witches. The largest factions of Hereditary/Traditional Witches are found in Europe, where the roots of the Wiccan tree are firmly planted. These Witches pass down their Craft within the family circle. Very rarely will they allow an outsider in and they usually only initiate within the bloodline.

Hereditary/Traditional Witches have a slightly different method of doing things than the post-Gardnerian Wiccans do. Generally, most do not use the standard set of magical tools, but rely on everyday items to serve as symbols of their craft. Importance is placed on nature deities, fertility, charms, amulets, and herbal potions. Full moons are generally used for divination and the working of magic, and seasonal celebrations focus on the prosperity and protection of the family unit.

Strega Wicca

Italian Witchcraft, called Stregheria or Strega, dates back to the 14th Century and is steeped in ancient folklore. It is believed that Strega descends from an ancient tribe that worshiped the moon and used nature and spirits to work its magic. The religion acknowledges the polarity of gender and personifies this in the form of God and Goddess. Their year is divided into the God months (October through February) and the Goddess months (March through September).

In keeping with tradition, the eight seasonal shifts are acknowledged and celebrated within a ritual context. The four tools of magic (wand, athame, chalice, and pentagram) are accepted as symbols of power and potential. Magic is considered to be an integral part of the religion, as are spells, omens, and charms. Talismans are used to manifest desire.

Strega recognizes a spiritual teacher in the form of Aridia, who is sent to earth to form a covenant with her followers. All those who follow Aridia and her Old Religion are blessed with insight and personal power. A great deal of importance is placed on lunar rites, star magic, and mythical prophecy.

Chapter 2

Principles of Wiccan Belief

"Man is born to believe. And if no Church comes forward with its title-deeds of truth...to guide him, he will find altars and idols in his own heart and his own imagination."
—Benjamin Disraeli

L ike most genuine forms of spirituality, Wicca creates a sense of security and stability within the believer. This sense of stability, of knowing there is something more to life than just the physical, brings promise for the future. When this sense of security is combined with a true love for deity, the void of the soul is filled and true peace of mind is found.

One of the most outstanding features of all religions is belief—belief in deity, sacred scripture, and ritual custom. Beliefs form the nucleus of all religious systems. They are the roots and trunk from which the religion grows and flourishes. Without strong beliefs, no religion can weather the tides of time.

Because Witchcraft is a child with many fathers, and the offspring of a thousand claimants, it is difficult to place the beliefs of one tradition above another. No one knows for sure where most of Wicca's doctrines actually come from, and to complicate matters, most contemporary Wiccans frequently disagree when it comes to religious matters.

However, there is one thing that most Wiccans and Pagans will agree on: The Principles of Wiccan Belief. These principles form the cornerstone of modern Wiccan belief, much as the Ten Commandments do for the Christian religion. The principles, which follow, were adopted by the Council of American Witches at their 1974 spring meet in Minneapolis. Most Wiccans still hold fast to these principles, even though the council disbanded shortly after its spring meet that year.

The Council of American Witches finds it necessary to define modern Witchcraft in terms of the American experience. We are not bound by traditions from other times and other cultures, and owe no allegiance to any person or power greater than the Divinity manifest throughout our own being. As American Witches, we welcome and respect all life-affirming teachings and traditions and seek to learn from all and to share our learning within our Council. We therefore ask that those who seek to identify with us accept these few basic principles.

Council Principles

1. We practice Rites to attune ourselves with the natural rhythm of life forces marked by the phases of the moon and the seasonal quarters and cross quarters.

2. We recognize that our intelligence gives us a unique responsibility toward our environment. We seek to live in harmony with Nature, in ecological balance offering fulfillment.

3. We acknowledge a depth of power far greater than is apparent to the average person. Because it is far greater than ordinary, it is sometimes called "supernatural," but we see it as lying within that which is naturally potential to all.

4. We conceive of the creative power of the Universe as manifesting through polarity – as masculine and feminine – and believe that this same creative power lives in all people and functions through the interaction of the masculine and feminine. We value neither above the other, knowing each to be supportive of the other. We value sex as pleasure, as the symbol and embodiment of life, and as one of the sources of energies used in magical practice and religious worship.

5. We recognize both outer worlds and inner, or psychological, worlds – sometimes known as the spiritual world, the collective unconscious, the Inner Planes, etc. – and we see in the interaction of these two dimensions the basis for paranormal phenomena and magical exercises. We neglect neither dimension for the other, seeing both as necessary for our fulfillment.

6. *We do not recognize any authoritarian hierarchy, but do honor those who teach, respect those who share their greater knowledge and wisdom, and acknowledge those who have courageously given of themselves in leadership.*

7. *We see religion, magic, and wisdom-in-living as being united in the way one views the world and lives within it – a worldview and philosophy of life that we identify as Witchcraft, the Wiccan Way.*

8. *Calling oneself a "witch" does not make a Witch – but neither does heredity itself, or the collecting of titles, degrees, and initiations. A Witch seeks to control the forces within him/herself that make life possible in order to live wisely and well, without harm to others, and in harmony with Nature.*

9. *We acknowledge that it is the affirmation and fulfillment of life, in a continuation of evolution and development of consciousness, that gives meaning to the Universe we know and to our personal role within it.*

10. *Our only animosity toward Christianity, or toward any other religion or philosophy of life, is to the extent that its institutions have claimed to be "the only way" and have sought to deny freedom to others and to suppress other ways of religious practice and belief.*

11. *As American Witches, we are not threatened by debates on the history of the Craft, the origins of various terms, or the legitimacy of various aspects of different traditions. We are concerned with our present and our future.*

12. *We do not accept the concept of "absolute evil," nor do we worship any entity known as "Satan" or "the devil," as defined by the Christian tradition. We do not seek power through the suffering of others, nor do we accept the concept*

that personal benefit can only be derived from denial to another.

13. We acknowledge that we seek within Nature that which is contributory to our health and well-being.

The Wiccan Rede

One of the nice things about Wicca is its live-and-let-live philosophy. There is room for everyone and for everyone's personal belief system. Most Wiccans consider it unethical to impose their beliefs on others, let alone tell them how they should worship. This mandate to tolerate and respect others is passed along to each new initiate in the form of the Wiccan Rede—the Wiccan golden rule.

The Wiccan Rede

Bide the Wiccan laws ye must, in perfect love and perfect trust.

Live and let live — fairly take and fairly give.

Cast the Circle thrice about to keep the evil spirits out.

To bind the spell every time, let the spell be spake in rhyme.

Soft of eye and light of touch — speak ye little, listen much.

Deosil go by the waxing moon — sing and dance the Wiccan Rune.

Widdershins go when the Moon doth wane, and the werewolf howls by the dread wolfsbane.

When the Lady's Moon is new, kiss the hand to Her times two.

When the Moon rides at Her peak, then your heart's desire seek.

Head the North wind's mighty gale — lock the door and drop the sail.

When the wind comes from the South, love will kiss thee on the mouth.

When the West wind blows o'er, the departed spirits restless be.

Nine woods in the Cauldron go, burn them quick and burn them slow.

Elder be ye Lady's tree — burn it not or cursed ye'll be.

When the Wheel begins to turn, let the Beltane fires burn.

When the Wheel has turned to Yule, light the log and let Pan rule.

Heed ye flower, bush, and tree — by the Lady blessed be.

When the rippling waters go, cast a stone and truth ye'll know.

When ye are in dire need, hearken not to others' greed.

With the fool no season spend, or be counted as his friend.

Mind the threefold law ye should — three times bad and three times good.

When misfortune is enow, wear the blue star on thy brow.

True in love ever be, unless thy lover's false to thee.

Eight words the Wiccan Rede fulfill, an ye harm none, do what ye will.

Traditional Coven Policy

The word "coven" usually conjures up visions of people all dressed in black, wildly dancing around a bubbling cauldron. While this picture is not necessarily without merit, it is not the sum total of Witchcraft or the Wiccan religion.

Although most Witches prefer to remain solitary (that is, to work alone), there are those who join covens, usually made up of 13 people, including a leader. The number 13 is considered lucky because it can't be divided against itself. This is, however, the ideal, and not the norm. Most groups have far fewer members.

One of the first things a new member is given upon joining a coven is a set of tenets, or coven laws. These laws have been drafted by the coven members for the purpose of maintaining order. They are usually based on common courtesy and good sense, two things most people seem to forget when emotions are involved.

The following laws were passed on to me when I was initiated more than 20 years ago. Whether you are a spiritual leader or a solitary practitioner, reasonable standards and ethics never go out of style.

The Laws

1.   Each group or tradition in Wicca has its own beliefs and ways. Each should follow according to its own path. So long as it harms none and respects the spirit of the universe, all traditions shall be viewed as equally valid under the God and Goddess.

2. We believe there is a supreme Force that created and maintains the universe and represents itself through the myriad of universal gods and goddesses. We acknowledge these gods and goddesses as whole and complete unto themselves and equal unto each other.

3. For our part, we do not fear to have a woman bring in a woman, nor a man bring in a man. It is better to have a wise teacher of the same sex than a fool of the opposite.

4. We view Wicca as an answer, not an excuse to avoid that which takes effort or may be emotionally hurtful.

5. For those who seek initiation, it should be remembered that initiation is an occurrence within the heart. The ceremony is only its restatement before the gods and those who represent them.

6. Within any organization there must be a leader or leaders. In Wicca we defer to a High Priestess and a High Priest. We also realize that there is no such thing as a perfect High Priest or High Priestess. The imperfections of our leaders should not be cause for disorder, but rather for understanding, tolerance, and love.

7. There comes a time in every family or coven when there must be a cessation of friendship. What one might refrain from saying to a friend or loved one, one might be obliged to say as a High Priest or High Priestess. Discipline is one such obligation.

8. You must remember you will never have the power of the teacher who trained you. This does not mean that you will never have the same amount of power as those who came before.

Power is not ability, and your ability may surpass all others'. Power is the ability to demand respect. You will never have the respect due to your teachers. Demand your own by controlling your ability.

9. Thinking of hurting is not the same as working to cause pain. Either action may be accomplished with little force of will, but with greater force of will, both can be avoided.

10. Those with knowledge and ability need not prove it. Those who fear their ability fear themselves. Fear has no place within the Craft of the Wise.

11. Express only that which you know. Work only within your realm of availability. Leave the fools unto themselves, and seek out those with truth in their hearts. Let not their words nor actions lead you but rather look to their works and deeds. Those speaking truth will be known by their works.

12. Observe and listen, and reserve judgment. For until the silver is weighed, who knows the weight.

13. Always treat others as you yourself wish to be treated. Remember that evil begets evil, but good begets joy and happiness.

Chapter 3

Wiccan Roots: The Celtic Druids

"To the peoples of antiquity, the isle of Britain was the very home and environment of mystery, a sacred territory. To enter was to encroach upon the region of enchantment, the dwelling of the gods."
—Lewis Spence, *The Mysteries of Britain*

To fully appreciate the Wiccan religion, one must understand its history. Wicca, as we know it today, evolved from the pre-Christian, Shamanic religious traditions of Europe, which were heavily influenced by the practices of Celtic Druids.

The Celts were a branch of the Indo-European people who migrated around 3000 B.C. from their homeland, west of the Black Sea, into Old Europe, a small region east of the Black Sea. They were a loosely knit group of tribes with a common culture and language. By about 400 B.C., they were recognizable as a distinct culture. The Celts were cattle herders, horse breeders, and head hunters (they took heads as war trophies). Short swords, lances, and chariots were some of their sophisticated war-making implements. Among their sports were fishing, hunting, and, of course, fighting — which they loved above all. They were not a docile, peaceful race, but rather aggressive, barbaric, and war-loving.

In general, the Celts were exceptionally tall and robust compared to the shorter and slighter Greeks and Romans, whose territory they invaded. Because of their size, tattoos, and blonde hair, the Celts must have seemed like strange giants to the civilized Romans. Even their clothing appeared odd, as both sexes generally dressed alike in breeches, knee-length tunics, and brightly colored cloaks. They adorned themselves with rings, bracelets, armlets, ornate buckles, and intricate gold and silver brooches that secured their cloaks.

The Celts were known for the fairness of their laws, which, among other things, guaranteed rights for women. In Celtic society, a woman could own property, choose a husband, and get a divorce. Women fought in battle alongside their husbands. If a woman's husband died, she took over his role as chief in their family line.

Within the Celtic tribe, or clan, there were three levels of recognition. First was the king, a descendent of a hero or warrior leader who was recognized for his prowess in battle. Next were the warriors, chosen for their ability to protect and defend the clan during times of attack. Last came the common people, who were the herders, farmers, and pro-ducers of the products needed for sustaining daily life.

Separate from the clan and yet a part of it were the Druid priests, the Celtic clergy. This special priesthood, like the tribe, was divided into three classes, each with its own functions and responsibilities. First in order was the Druid/ Derwydd, who was adviser to the chief or king and acted as judge and lawyer to the people. He also held authority in worship and ritual. Next were the Ovates/Ovydd, who were the priests and priestesses in charge of prophecy and divi-nation. In the last grade were the Bards/Bardd, who were poets, musicians, and keepers of tradition. They were trained in music, history, and song-spell. An Arch-Druid ruled all three groups. The senior brethren (those considered the most learned) elected the Arch-Druid by lot.

The Celtic cosmology and Druid spiritual system were based on the fundamental belief in the Law of Three (or the Logical Order of the Triad), which was the association of humans with nature combined with divinity. This produced a religious system that was monotheistic in its underlying creed (Druids believed in one creator), but polytheistic in its ritualistic practices (they worshipped many gods and goddesses). Prior to Christianity, this dualistic approach toward religion was common, especially in agricultural and livestock-breeding cultures. Because of their association with the land and animals, these people were more aware of the subtle energies and power potential of natural phenomena.

The Druids unfortunately did not keep written records of their spiritual practices. Most of what we know about them comes from the records of their conquerors and the myths and legends of the bards.

Basic Beliefs and Practices of Celtic Druids

Three Aspects in One

The Druidic faith of the Celts centered on one supreme creative force, which manifested itself through:

1. **Divinity:** The gods, goddesses, angels, and nature spirits.
2. **Nature:** Including the elements (Earth, Air, Fire, and Water), as well as places where energy was present, such as caves, rivers, wells, mountains, tree groves, and the ocean.
3. **Animated Existence:** Humanity, animals, birds, fish, and all living creatures great and small.

Spiral of Abred

Druids believed in reincarnation, as expressed in the Spiral of Abred, the circle of creation. This was the great circle on which the cycle of life moved like a wheel from birth to death and then back again. Each life allowed for more experience to be gained in order to elevate the individual's spirit closer to its original source.

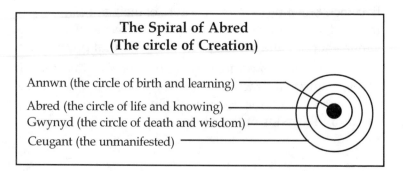

The Spiral of Abred
(The circle of Creation)

Annwn (the circle of birth and learning)
Abred (the circle of life and knowing)
Gwynyd (the circle of death and wisdom)
Ceugant (the unmanifested)

Belief in reincarnation or an afterlife was very important to tribal people. Living conditions were less than comfortable, but they believed that with effort and work, one could almost guarantee a position in the afterlife and progress in lifetimes to come.

The Transcendent Three

As with every aspect of their lives, the Druids' view of the deity was expressed in a triad, known as the transcendent three. The reason for their belief in threes was the fact that it takes two to create a third, which contains elements of the original components and is at the same time unique.

The first principle of the triad was the employment of God to lighten the darkness, invest nonentity with a body, and animate the dead. The second principle was the employment or duty of God to express will, wisdom, and love. The third principle was the expression of God that stated there were three things beyond the human realm: the extreme limits of space, the beginning and end of time, and the work of God.

The Five Forces of Influence

The Druids also honored anything of natural importance. Nowhere was this more evident than in their Five Forces of Influence:

1. Influence of place.
2. Richness of time.
3. Treasures of tribe.
4. Glory of ancestors.
5. Joy of journey.

The Four Elements

The Celtic culture was based on agriculture and livestock breeding, which no doubt influenced the religious customs and practices of the Druids. Because of their dependence on the land and the herd, Druids recognized the four elements and seasonal changes as being of great consequence. As with most early peoples, everything that affected the tribe—including the weather—had some sort of mystical significance.

The four Elements and their corresponding symbols of the land:

Air	*Slea Blue (the spear).*
Fire	*Cliamh Solis (the sword).*
Water	*Cauldron of the Dagada.*
Earth	*Lia Fail (the stone of destiny).*

As a pastoral people, the Celts had great respect for the land and all that rose from the soil. From their appreciation for the bounty of Mother Earth came their observance of seasonal rites. In the eyes of the Celts, planning, planting, and harvesting were parts of life that could be governed through ritual observance. Their legacy of celebration is still with us today in the form of the eight Sabbats that make up the Wiccan Wheel of the Year.

Wheel of the Year

Samhain/Hallowmas:

October 31, the union of the worlds of spirit and man, the slaughter of the animals for winter food, and the beginning of rest. The Celtic New Year's Eve.

Alban Arthuan/Winter Solstice:

December 21, the death and rebirth of the sun, the lowest point of the sun, and the prayers for the return of the sun.

Imbolc/Candlemas:

February 1, the time of natural beginnings and preparation for the growing season.

Alban Eiler/Spring Equinox:

March 21, the time of fertile ground, when planting begins; also the time of equal day and night.

Beltane/May Day:

May 1, the time of fertility, when both animals and land were ready for impregnation by seed.

Alban Heruin/Summer Solstice:

June 21, the highest point of the sun, the time to nurture the young and appreciate the eternally moving circle.

Lughnasadh/Lammas:

August 1, the marriage of light and fire, the baking of the first loaf, and the beginning of the harvest.

Alban Elude/Autumnal Equinox:

September 21, the time of ripened achievement and equal day and night; also known as the harvest home.

Sacred Symbol

The Druids, like members of many religions and spiritual traditions, had a symbol that expressed their philosophy in a simple form. This sacred symbol consisted of three columns, each of which corresponded to one of the letters O, I, and U. These mystical letters and corresponding lines represented the three attributes of God:

1. Love (O)   2. Knowledge (I)   3. Truth (U)

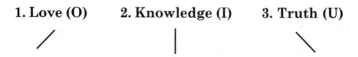

The Nemeton

Because of the Druids' relationship with the land, they did not believe that God should be housed in a building. Thus they practiced their faith in what was called a Nemeton, sacred ground that had been consecrated for spiritual use. For added power and energy, the Nemeton was set in a grove of trees, upon a hill, or near a sacred well.

The Nemeton was surrounded by a bank and a ditch with water, somewhat like a miniature moat. Oftentimes poles with the heads of sacrificed victims were placed around the perimeter of the Nemeton. Inside the border of the Nemeton there was a sacred fire pit, an altar stone, and a shaft or well for votive deposits. The shape of the Nemeton may have been important as well. It is believed that the rectangular Nemetons were dedicated to the Gods, and that circular ones were dedicated to the Goddess. Situated on a hilltop, deep within the forest, or beside a babbling brook, the Nemeton was sacred space consecrated to the work of the Old Gods.

The influence of both the Druids and Celtic culture on Western culture cannot be ignored. The Druids left a rich heritage of symbolism, celebration, and worship. The most recognized of their customs are the seasonal celebrations. The Druid festival of Samhain became All Hallows' Eve, which we now celebrate as Halloween. The fertility festival of Beltane became May Day. Carving pumpkins, kissing under the mistletoe, Easter egg hunting, and May pole dancing were all passed down to us from our Celtic ancestors.

As the priests of the Celtic people, the Druids taught belief in the soul's eternal nature and that all forms of creation contain a living spirit. According to an ancient Druid saying, "Spirit sleeps in the mineral, breathes in the vegetable, dreams in the animal, and wakes in man." The Druids also believed the soul could be contacted after death and that eventually the soul would reincarnate.

The Druids had a practical approach to living in harmony with the world around them. If we embrace their ways, we learn to respect nature, God, and the creative force within. It is through the symbolism, seasonal rites, and worship of the Old Gods that Celtic Wicca is able to celebrate the Druids' philosophy and way of life. With some modification and creative mixing, this beginner's guide can help you create a Wiccan tradition of your very own. And even though some will say that Wicca and Druidry are two separate and distinct entities, they nevertheless complement each other and offer themselves as alternatives to mainstream religious thought.

Chapter 4

Deity: The God and Goddess

"Divinity is in its omniscience and omnipotence like a wheel, like a circle, a whole, that can neither be understood, nor divided, nor begun, nor ended."
—Illustrations of Hildegard of Bingen

Wicca is a very individualized religion, in which each person chooses his or her own deities to worship. Generally, the supreme being is considered to be a genderless energy source like The Force in the *Star Wars* trilogy. This force is referred to as the All and is comprised of many different aspects of the Universe. These aspects are reflected in the masculine and feminine forces of nature, which appear in the guise of the world's different gods and goddesses.

People just getting interested in Wicca often wonder just who or what the Pagan gods are. Are they images of the human mind created by our ancestors? Are they archetypal images of the collective human unconscious? Are they planetary spirits that rule all life on Earth, or cosmic forces that antedate the human race? The answer is not a simple one, and must be discovered for oneself through training and experience.

This individual freedom to ponder and pursue that which comes from within is what makes Witchcraft such a unique experience. There is no pressure to adopt another person's idea or concept of deity. There is no one, true, right, and only way. Each person is considered to be responsible for his or her own spiritual growth, development, and relationship with deity.

The God

Like all deities, the God has many faces. He appears as the radiant, brilliant, and illuminating Sun of Righteousness, the divine victim who spills his blood for the love of the land, and the warrior king whose fight for truth and justice are revealed in the battle between good and evil. To all those who practice Wicca, the God is the symbol of virility, the fertilizing and regenerating energy force of nature. He is the personification of all that is masculine, potent, and powerful.

The God's most obvious and dominant characteristic is his ability to regenerate. Although his countenance may change with time and culture, he continually returns to live and die for the land he loves. He has been known as Osiris, Tammuz, and Adonis. He has manifested as the Unconquered Sun or compassionate savior Mithra and Helios. Whatever his incarnation, he is always the potentate of power, strength, and authority—and the final judge before the gate of the Goddess.

The Sun God

In Wicca the presence of the divine is perceived in all aspects of nature. One of the most venerated natural phenomena is that of the sun. This radiant ball of fire provides light, brings forth life, and promotes healing. In addition to its timekeeping qualities, an important aspect of life, it has long symbolized the God.

The Sun God was believed to rule the sky and all that moved below it during the daylight hours. He presided over time, agriculture, war, fertility, and the regeneration of life. In the Romano-Celtic phase of Old Europe, the sun god was seen as being in a constant battle with the forces of darkness and evil. To aid the Sun God in his struggle against the powers of darkness, people worshiped him during early morning rituals. It was believed that these rituals would give him strength and help bring back his radiance each day.

The Horned God

Of all the god forms acknowledged by our Pagan ancestors, the Horned God was probably the most widely worshiped. Originally he was venerated through the physical manifestation of the stag, bull, and ram. Just like his animal counterpart, the Horned God was respected for his strength, vigor, beauty, swift movement, and protective capabilities. He represented the untamed forces of nature, and the ability to regenerate life. It wasn't until the advent of Christianity that he became the object of scorn, relegated to the level of evil, and the source of all human suffering.

One of the most widely recognized Horned Gods is Cernunnos, whose name means horned or peaked one. The most striking features of Cernunnos is his semi-zoomorphic form and ability to shape-shift. His close affinity with the stag is demonstrated by his adoption of antlers and hooves. His other ally is the snake, which wraps itself around his body and represents his ability to regenerate. In Old Europe, Cernunnos was considered to be The Lord of Animals (domestic and wild); dispenser of fruit, grain or money; and the god of fertility and abundance.

Today the prominence of the Horned God's position in Wicca is both understandable and appropriate. Because Wicca is a nature-based religion, it is only reasonable that its deities should reflect the awesome powers of the Universe. To many, these primal powers are reflected in the fertile Earth Mother and the magnificent Lord of the Hunt. These archetypal forces are perceived to contribute to the rhythms through which life, death, and rebirth echo eternally.

The Harvest God

The god of vegetation presided over the agricultural community as the son and lover of the Great Earth Mother. He was personified in the Middle East as Tammuz, in Egypt as Osiris, and throughout Old Europe as Dionysus and Adonis.

In ancient myths, the dying and returning god, as depicted in harvest rites, provided a means of salvation. To become part of his mystery tradition was to ensure for oneself a place within the framework of the afterlife. To some extent, the Lord of the Harvest represents an understanding of the sacral unity all humans needed to feel toward their labors in the field. It was this understanding of the powers of nature that sustained their communities and their sense of belonging.

To many of our ancestors, the harvest was a time of both celebration and mourning. The abundance of grain and wine were cause for great joy. On the other hand, the passing of the young God, hero, and lover of the Goddess was a time of great sorrow. The ancient myths of Tammuz and Ishtar, Isis and Osiris, and Aphrodite and Adonis best communicate this powerful drama of life, death, and return — all products of the harvest. This continuous cycle of growing, dying, and returning was the foundation of the Pagan mysteries that predate Christianity. It is also the primary focus of most modern Wiccan traditions.

Selected Wiccan Gods

Apollo: Greek Lord of Light. The slayer of darkness, leader of the Muses, considered to be the shield against evil and champion of right. Apollo's symbols include the silver bow, laurel wreath, lyre, tripod, and golden throne of truth.

Cernunnos: Celtic Horned God. He was the god of nature, the underworld, and the astral plane. The priesthood of the Celts, the Druids, referred to him as Hu Gadarn, the horned god of fertility. The symbols for Cernunnos are the torc (Celtic neck-ring), horns, spear, serpent, shield, and cornucopia.

Dionysus: Greek Horned God. Dionysus was a savior god. He was twice born, and considered to be the Lion of Light. Dionysus was the youthful victim, priest of night, lord of the dance, wine, and bringer of ecstasy. The vine, drum, phallus, ivy wreath, and thyrsus (*wood wand or staff tipped with a pine cone shaped ornament*) were some of his symbols.

Faunus: Roman Horned God. Faunus was a pastoral god, primarily of the forests, a hunter and promoter of agriculture. He was equated with the Greek god Pan. His symbols were the club, drinking horn, crown, and panther skin.

Lugh: Celtic God of Light. Lugh was known as the shining one and was considered to be a war god of great skill. He was a god of arts, crafts, commerce, blacksmiths, poets, and bards. His symbols include the rod-sling, spear, white stag, and forge.

Osiris: Egyptian Agriculture God. Osiris, one the most popular of the Egyptian deities, was a god of vegetation and nature and represented the ability to regenerate. He was the patron of fertility and the harvest. His symbols include the crook, flail, scepter, and all agricultural tools.

Ra: Egyptian Sun God. Ra was also called the Great One, the Old One, the Father of the Gods, and the Lord of Light. He was respected as the self-generator/creator, the breath of all life, and the divine love and radiant power of the universe. His image was of a hawk-headed man wearing a solar disk. His symbols include the sun, the scepter, and a boat.

Sol: Roman, the Invincible Sun. Sol was the inspirer of prophecy, seer of hidden truth, and bestower of the vital force. Sol surveys all that is in the tangible world and knows all that lies in the hidden worlds. Sol was represented by the crown of seven rays, the cornucopia, horses, swans, and the laurel crown.

Tammuz: Assyro-Babylonian. God of Vegetation and the Harvest. Tammuz was in love with the goddess Ishtar and was killed and transported to the underworld. Ishtar went to look for him and the world was left barren until her return. Tammuz's symbols were the flute, wand, bread, and boar, and he was honored in small gardens.

When working with Wiccan gods, keep in mind primary characteristics: The Sun God represents youth, beauty, and enlightenment; the Horned God represents maturity, masculinity, and lust; and the Harvest God represents wisdom, protection, guardianship of the land, and continual regeneration.

The Goddess

After centuries of exile, the goddess has made her way back to her land, people, and position as the personification of feminine dominion and perception. She is the Earth Mother and Mistress of Magic; she is all that is beauty and bounty. What the God inaugurates, the Goddess realizes. He impregnates her with the seed of desire and she gives birth to reality. The Goddess is the creative process through which all physical levels are manifested.

The Goddess is the intuitive and instinctive side of nature. Her inconceivable powers of transition and transformation radiate like translucent beams of celestial light, for she is the mystery and magic. Beneath her full, round moon she has been, and still is, invoked as Arianrhod, Diana, and Hecate by those seeking her favors. Everything psychic and mysterious belongs to her alone.

The Moon Goddess

It was the moon that lit the way for early humans. The moon glowed in the night sky. Its light helped guide hunters, warriors, and travelers safely through the dark and back to their tribes.

As our ancestors looked to the heavens, they saw how the moon waxed and waned, how night turned into day, spring into summer, and summer into winter. They saw the seas ebb and flow, plants bring forth grain, and life burst forth from the womb. Everything in nature seemed to move in harmony with the phases of the moon, including women's menstrual cycles and pregnancy. The Great Goddess worshiped in Old Europe became equated with the moon, in whose divine light she was reflected. As the moon waxed and waned, so did the inherent power of the Goddess.

The waxing moon was perceived as the Maiden aspect of the goddess, the virgin in charge of her own life, true to her own nature, and under the influence of none. This was the time of dreams, challenges, and spiritual potential.

When the moon reached its full, pregnant glory, it was perceived as the Mother. Here we find the nurturer, the giver of life and bringer of death, the Goddess's most powerful, and certainly most venerated phase. This was the time of great fertility and increased psychic awareness. It was a time usually set aside to visualize and formulate physical desires.

The waning moon saw the decline of light and was associated with the Crone, who symbolized the manifestation process and was associated with wisdom. What was conceived on the full moon was realized during the waning moon. This was also a time of contemplation and realization of personal accomplishments.

Once the moon completes its three major phases, it passes into a period of transition known as the New Moon. This three day period was, and still is, considered the time of the Enchantress or Temptress—a time of great mystery and magic.

The Mother Goddess

The Mother Goddess is an extremely complex image, as well as one of the most powerful figures within the Wiccan religion. She is the epitome of feminine beauty, fertility, and the ability to nurture. In Pagan times the Mother Goddess ruled over the fecundity of humans and animals, and was often referred to as the Lady or Mother of Beasts.

To our Pagan ancestors, the Mother Goddess was both loved and feared. She was the serene benefactor in charge of life, fertility, and regeneration. As the Great Mother she brought forth life, and as the Terrible Mother she ruled over death and destruction. It was because of this duality that the Mother Goddess was associated with the powers of light and darkness.

Throughout Old Europe the Mother Goddess embraced a wide range of activities. Besides her affiliation with fertility, she was also the embodiment of maturity and abundance. To express these qualities, images of the Mother Goddess were endowed with large breasts, swollen bellies, and full buttocks.

The concept of nurturing, with its ability to transcend the harsh realities of life and express unconditional love, brings many people to the Goddess of Wicca. Once they are embraced by the Mother Goddess, their connection to the potential of the manifestation process is reawakened. When this happens, people become able to connect with their own nurturing potential, which develops spiritual maturity.

In the Wiccan religion, to invoke the Mother Goddess is to awaken the primeval feminine nature within. The essence of the Goddess is then able to penetrate the very fiber of the individual, opening his or her mind, heart, and soul to all that is love, life, and wisdom. The act of invoking the Mother Goddess unites the senses with the ultimate feminine power and force of all creation.

The Triple Goddess

The Triple Goddess can be found in almost all mythologies. She is at once virgin, mother, and crone, the waxing, full, and waning moons. She represents all that is feminine, enchanting, ripe, and wise. In the ancient mystery traditions, the Triple Goddess was associated with water, weaving, and war. Some of the best examples of her threefold nature can be found in Greek, Celtic, and Norse mythology.

The Greeks envisioned the Triple Goddess in the form of the Moirae or Fates. They were born from the great goddess Nyx and belong to the earliest stratum of divinities. They were known as the Spinners of Fate, who spun out the days of human life as if they were yarn. The length of this yarn was decided entirely by them. Even the great god Zeus could not go against their decrees.

Brigid is the major triple goddess in Celtic mythology. She had three distinct facets: poetry, smithing, and healing. She brought inspiration to those who worked with music and poetry. She aided those who crafted metal and weapons by working with fire. She also nourished those who brought comfort to the sick by giving them the power to heal.

In Norse mythology, the Triple Goddess appeared as the Norns or Wyrd Sisters. They were known as the Urd (past), Verdandi (present), and Skuld (future). They were the spinners who sat at the well of Urd, which was located at the roots of the World Tree, Yggdrasil. Because they came from the earliest of times they were able to dispense their fate upon gods and humans alike.

The triplicity of the Goddess is an important concept within the Wiccan Religion. In her manifestation as the Virgin, the Goddess has no connection with the masculine. However, when she ripens into the Mother, the Goddess becomes a faithful wife or the harlot who takes on many lovers. With the passage of time her fertility wanes, but not her life experience. Thus, the Goddess is transformed into the Crone of knowledge and wisdom. It is through the understanding of these three aspects of the Goddess—birth, life, and death—that we learn to nourish and sustain our own inner resources.

Selected Wiccan Goddesses

Brigid: Celtic Triple Goddess. She is the embodiment of poetry, inspiration, and divination. Brigid was originally a sun and fire goddess known as Brigid of the Golden Hair. Because of her connection with fire, Brigid was associated with inspiration and the art of smith craft. Brigid was also an important fertility goddess. She was called on during birth to protect the mother and the child. Brigid's symbols include the spindle, flame, well, ewe/lamb, milk, snake, and bell.

Cerridwen: Celtic Mother Goddess. Cerridwen, associated with Astarte or Demeter, is the mother goddess of the moon and grain. She is especially known for her fearsome death totem, a white, corpse-eating sow. Cerridwen's harvest celebrations express her ability to both give and take away life. Her symbols include the cauldron, cup, sow, and hound.

Diana: Roman Moon Goddess: She was the patroness of hunters and guardian of the forest where her sacred grove stood near Aricia. In Rome, she joined with Janus, a god of light and the sun, serving as a consort depicting the light of the moon. Diana's symbols include the bow and arrow, sandals, magical weapons, the dog, and the stag.

Demeter: Greek Earth Mother. As the goddess of vegetation, she was founder of agriculture and the civic rite of marriage. Her mysteries, called the "Thesmophoria," were held each April and her cult center was at Eleusis, south of Athens. Demeter's symbols include the basket, scepter, torch, water jug, sheaf of wheat, and cow.

Hecate: Greek Triple Moon Goddess. To the Greeks, Hecate was one of the oldest embodiments of the triple moon goddess. She held the power over the heavens, earth, and the underworld, where she was in control of birth, life, and death. Hecate was the giver of visions, magic, and regeneration. Hecate's symbols include the key, rope, double-edged dagger, cross triangle, besom, crossroads, hound, and torch.

Isis: Egyptian Mother Goddess: Isis is the personification of the Great Goddess in her aspect of maternal devotion. Isis was probably the greatest goddess in Egypt and was worshiped for more than 3,000 years. Her influence was not confined to Egypt and spread to Greece and the Roman Empire. Isis was the female principle of nature and therefore a goddess of a thousand names. Isis's symbols include the Thet (knot or buckle), scepter, cup, horns, mirror, snake, and girdle.

Rhea: Cretan Mother Goddess: Her name probably means Earth, and she was usually depicted as a huge, stately woman surrounded by animals and small, subservient human males. Rhea was incorporated into Greek myth as a Titan, one of the second generation of deities. She was recognized as the goddess of the living earth. Rhea's symbols include the torch, brass drum, double ax, and fruit bearing trees.

The Morrigan: Celtic Triple Goddess: The Morrigan is the terrible hag goddess of Celtic legend. She bears some relationship to the Furies and Valkyries of Norse Myth. She appears as a triple goddess of battle and depicts the harsh, unrelenting warrior side of the Celtic soul. The Morrigan's symbols include the raven, crow, battle ax, shield, and spear.

When working with Wiccan goddesses, keep in mind primary characteristics: Moon Goddess represents spiritual illumination and is the essence of magic and mystery; Mother Goddess represents the sensual/nurturing side of the feminine nature and is filled with grace; and Triple Goddess exemplifies enchantment, seductiveness, and wisdom.

Seasons of the God and Goddess

Wicca, like all mystery traditions, relies heavily on symbolism. When a person views a symbol, his or her consciousness is automatically elevated to a realm of higher perception and understanding. Religious art, objects, and charts are used to create a bridge between the conscious and unconscious minds. They both reveal and veil certain realities and truths according to each individual's level of understanding.

The Seasons of the God and Goddess chart, which follows, is a good example of symbolic illustration. Looking at the chart, one immediately grasps the relationship between time and deity. Whereas the Goddess maintains a very restrained and controlled position within the seasonal cycle, the God is more independent, less confined, and not as directly involved with cyclic change. It is generally accepted that feminine energy is more influential and intimately involved with the cycles of nature than masculine energy is, even thought the latter does have a dominating effect.

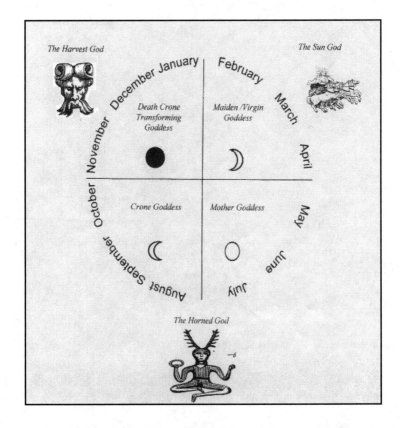

Chapter 5

Wiccan Myth and Scripture

"Myth is an attempt to narrate a whole human experience, of which the purpose is too deep, going too deep in the blood and soul, for the mental explanation or description."
—D.H. Lawrence

W ithin the framework of the Wiccan religion there are many sacred texts. Some of these texts come from ancient sources and others are modern writings. Their purpose is to express the essential nature of the religion and its relation to human life. Most religions rely on the power of myth to impart spiritual wisdom.

Sacred myth provides us with a means of explaining our innermost thoughts and convictions. Through tales about long forgotten gods and heroes, the concepts of creation, love, and survival are brought to life. A good example is The Myth of Esus and Tarvos (reprinted here from my book *Reclaiming the Power*, Llewellyn Publications, 1992), wherein the cycles of life are explained through the concept of nature and seasonal change.

The Myth of Esus and Tarvos

Long ago when the world was young, a marvelous and wonderful thing happened. In the early spring, near the well of Coventina, a beautiful bull calf was born. At first glance you could see that it was not an ordinary bull. His coat was golden red and his form was perfect. His eyes were clear and bright and intelligent.

The bull was no sooner up and about, running and playing, when out of the sky descended three stately cranes. They danced about him in a circle, delighted with his beauty and energy. The bull was happy too. He liked his new friends who could sing and dance and fly. He was respectful of them too and bowed his head, for he knew they had come from the Great Sky Father.

As spring wore on into early summer, the bull grew exceedingly fast and was soon fully grown. Never was there a bull like this one. His fame spread far and wide. Animals, men, and gods came to look upon his great beauty. The cranes were his constant companions, and because of this, the bull became known as Tarvos Trigaranus (bull with three cranes).

Their days were those of endless enjoyment. The world was bright and beautiful and full of flowers. For in the ancient times the world had never known the winter.

Now, there was a hunter God named Esus (lord-master). He roamed through fields and forests looking for an animal worthy of his passion, but he found none to be of satisfaction. Early one beautiful morning, he happened upon the meadow where Tarvos and the three cranes were sleeping. One glance at the bull and Esus new his search had ended. He drew his blade and came upon the sleeping bull, but the cranes saw the danger and gave out the cry of alarm.

The bull rose to do battle with Esus and his horns were formidable weapons. The god Esus and the divine bull Tarvos clashed in combat. They fought all day and all night but neither could seem to beat the other. The contest continued in this manner for days.

Then, on the night of the dark of the moon, the bull began to fail in strength. And there, under the great Oak tree, Esus struck Tarvos, the divine bull, a deadly blow. His blood poured out upon the roots of the tree and its leaves turned golden-red at that very instant for pure shame and grief.

The cranes made a great crying sound. One of them flew forward and in a small dish caught up some of the bull's blood. Then the cranes departed, flying south.

A gloom descended upon the world. The flowers wilted and the trees dropped their leaves. The great sun withdrew its warmth. The world grew dark and cold and snow fell for the first time.

All man and beast prayed to the Great Earth Mother to bring back the warmth, or all would soon perish. She heard, and took pity on all of nature, and soon the light began to return.

The three cranes came flying back from the south, and one still had the dish. It flew to the great oak tree where Tarvos, the divine bull, had been slain. The crane then poured the blood upon the ground and suddenly out of the dust sprang a bull-calf, reborn from the Great Earth Mother.

All nature rejoiced. The warmth of the sun returned. Grass and flowers sprang up. The leaves budded out on the trees. Thus spring came again to the world.

In time, the hunter god Esus heard of the bull's rebirth and sought to find him. This was the beginning of the cycle that even to this day persists. Esus, the hunter god, ever overcomes the divine bull, but our Great Mother Earth ever causes him to be reborn.

And so it is with all of nature, the spring brings forth life, the summer makes it strong, the fall causes it to weaken, and the winter brings its death. We cannot control it or change it, but we can learn to understand and work with it.

The Descent of the Goddess

The following myth, The Descent of the Goddess, also known as The Myth of the Goddess, was passed down to Gerald Gardner in secret. (Inspired by *Arcadia, Gospel of The Witches,* first published in 1890 by Charles G. Leland, the *Myth of the Goddess* is believed to be a modern adaptation of the Ancient Greek myth, and Homeric Hymn, Demeter and Persephone.) Gardner believed it to be one of the more significant teachings within Witchcraft. It expresses the popular religious concept of relinquishment — the surrendering of the self for enlightenment. As the Goddess descends into the underworld, she must shed her physical garments, symbols of her physical identity. In return she is instructed in the mysteries of birth, life, death, and return.

In ancient times, our Lord, the Horned One, was (as he still is) the Controller, the Comforter. But men knew him as the dread Lord of the Shadows, lonely, stern, and just. But Our Lady the Goddess would solve all mysteries, even the mystery of death, so she journeyed to the underworld. Here the Guardian of the Portals challenged her:

"Strip off thy garments, lay aside thy jewels; for naught mayest thou bring with thee into this our land."

So she laid down her garments and her jewels, and was bound, as all living things must be who seek to enter the realms of Death, the Mighty One. Such was her beauty that Death himself knelt, and laid his sword and crown at her feet, and kissed her feet, saying:

"Blessed be thy feet that have brought thee in these ways. Abide with me; but let me place my cold hands upon your heart." And she replied: "I love thee not. Why dost thou cause all things that I love, and take delight in, to fade and die?" "Lady," replied Death, "it is age and fate, against which I am helpless. Age causes all things to wither, but men die at the end of time, I give them rest and peace and strength, so that they may return. But you, you are lovely. Return not, abide with me."

But she answered: "I love thee not." Then said Death: "If you will not receive my hand upon your heart, you must kneel to Death's scourge." "It is fate; better so," she said, and kneeled. And Death scourged her tenderly. And she cried: "I know the pangs of love." And Death raised her, and said, "Blessed be." And he gave her the five-fold salute, saying: "Thus only may you attain to joy and knowledge." And he taught her all his mysteries, and gave her the necklace that is the circle of rebirth. And she taught him her mystery of the sacred cup, which is the cauldron of rebirth.

They loved and were one, for there be three great mysteries in the life of man, and magick controls them all. To fulfill love, you must return again at the same time and at the same place as the loved ones, and you must meet, and know, and remember, and love them again.

But to be reborn, you must die, and be made ready for a new body. And to die, you must be born; and without love you may not be born.

And our Goddess is ever to love and bestow mirth and happiness, as she guards and cherishes all her children in life. In death she teaches the way to her communion, and even in this world she teaches the mystery of the Magick

Circle, which is placed between the world of men and the realm of the gods.

The Charge of the Goddess

One of the most widespread texts associated with the Wiccan religion is the Charge of the Goddess Inspired by *Arcadia, Gospel of The Witches*, Doreen Valiente composed Charge of the Goddess for use in Gardnerian rituals. The Charge was originally composed by Doreen Valiente for use in Gardnerian rituals. It became so popular that it was soon incorporated into the rituals and the teachings of most Wiccan traditions. As with most mythical scripture that survives across time and place, there are many personal interpretations and variations of the original. Though the following Charge of the Goddess may vary somewhat from the original text, the original intent and message are still intact.

Whenever ye have need of anything, once in the month, and better it be when the moon is full, then shall ye gather in a secret place and adore me, the Mother of the Stars, Eternal Maiden, and Queen of all Witcheries. There shall ye assemble, who are intent to learn of my mysteries, and who have not yet won my deepest secrets. And under my watchful eye will ye be taught that which is unknown.

To the glory of all creation, sing, feast, dance, make music, and love all in my presence. For mine is the ecstasy of the spirit, and mine is also the joy on earth, for my law is love unto all beings.

I beseech thee to keep pure your highest ideals, strive ever towards them, let none stop ye or turn ye aside. For mine is the secret that opens the door of youth, mine is the cup of wine of life, and mine is the Cauldron of Cerridwen – the Holy Grail of immortality.

I am the gracious Goddess, who gives the gift of joy unto the heart of man. When ye gather in my name I shall give thee knowledge of the spirit eternal, and beyond death I grant thee peace and freedom, and in time union with those who have gone before.

Hear now the words of the Star Goddess, whose body encircles the universe. I am the beauty of the green earth, and the white moon amongst the stars, and the mystery of the waters, and the desire of all men.

I call unto your soul to arise and come unto me, for I am the soul of all nature who giveth life unto the universe. From me all things proceed, and unto me all things must return. Beloved of the gods and men, let my innermost divine self be molded in the raptures of the infinite. Let my worship be within thy heart, for rejoice, all acts of love and pleasure are my rituals.

Therefore, let there always be beauty and strength, power and compassion, honor and humility, mirth and reverence within ye. And thee who seek me out, know that seeking and yearning shall avail thee not, unless thou knowest the mystery. For that which thou seek, if thou shall not find it within, thou will never find it without. For behold, I have been with thee from the beginning and I am that which is attained at the end of desire. Remember this, as it shall light the way, and lead you unto thine most holy of all mysteries.

The Witches' Chant

Simple, direct, and intuitive, "The Witches' Chant" evokes a time when Wiccans and Pagans explained their mysteries in poetic verse. This particular chant was first revealed to the public in 1974 in *The Grimoire of Lady Sheba,* who was an honorary Gardnerian and Hereditary Witch. Although her book has been out of print for several decades, her teachings are still considered to be of great value and part of Wiccan history.

Through poetic verse, "The Witches' Chant" details the beliefs and practices of the ancient, matrifocal Witch Cult of Old Europe. The four quarters and the moon are evoked, tools are set upon an altar, and magic rites are enacted before the Queen of Heaven and the Horned Hunter.

Darksome night and shining moon,
Harken to the Witches Rune.
East then South, West then North
Hear! Come! I call thee forth.

By all the powers of Land and Sea,
Be obedient unto me.
Wand, and Pentacle, and Sword,
Harken ye unto my word.

Cords and Censer, Scourge and Knife,
Waken all into life.
Powers of the Witches' Blade,
Come ye as the charge is made.

Queen of Heaven, Queen of Hell
Send your aid unto this spell.
Horned Hunter of the night,
Work my will by magic rite.

By all the powers of Land and Sea,
As I do say, "so mote it be."
By all the might of Moon and Sun
As I do will, it shall be done.

Invocation for Drawing Down the Moon

It was believed by the ancient Greeks and Romans that Witches had the power to draw down the moon from the sky. This assumption is not without reason — were the Witch to be seen invoking the Goddess beneath a full moon, she would naturally be standing in a position where the beams from the moon would highlight her person, making it seem as if she had a direct link to the lunar orb.

In modern Wicca, the rite of Drawing Down the Moon (or Calling Down the Moon) is of considerable importance. During this potent invocation, the practitioner enters a trance-like state of altered consciousness and draws the essence of the Goddess into herself. The energy of the Goddess is then used for a magical act, for divining the future, or for spiritual revelation.

The act of Drawing Down the Moon involves being completely open and receptive to the feminine spirit of nature. It is usually done out of doors. Beneath a full moon, the practitioner stands with arms outstretched, palms pointing upward towards the moon. Once relaxed and focused on the moon, the practitioner slowly begins the following invocation, building to an emotional climax.

> *Bewitching Goddess of the cross roads*
> *Whose secrets are kept in the night,*
> *You are half remembered, half forgotten*
> *And are found in the shadows of night.*
>
> *From the misty hidden caverns*
> *In ancient magic days,*
> *Comes the truth once forbidden*
> *Of thy heavenly veiled ways.*

Cloaked in velvet darkness
A dancer in the flames
You who are called Diana, Hecate,
And many other names.

I call upon your wisdom
And beseech thee from this time,
To enter my expectant soul
That our essence shall combine.

I beckon thee O Ancient One
From far and distant shore,
Come, come be with me now
This I ask, and nothing more.

The sacred texts presented here express the essential nature of the Wiccan religion. They also help establish it as a viable spiritual philosophy with its own unique mythological history. The important thing to focus on when reading sacred text is how it makes you feel, not when it was written. Despite the fact that most Wiccan doctrine is less than seventy-five years old, it still brings hope, personal empowerment, and enlightenment to the devotee. And, after all, isn't that what matters?

Chapter 6

The Four Elements

"Nature, as a whole and in all its elements, enunciates something that may be regarded as an indirect self-communication of God to all those ready to receive it."
—Martin Buber, *At The Turning*

T he world we live in is a combination of many forces, all working together to maintain life. These forces are comprised of both physical and metaphysical (spiritual) elements, which are fundamental to the creation process and essential for supporting life as we know it. We need to understand these principal forces if we are to understand the universe and the dynamic energy that controls it.

The principle forces are the four elements: Air, Fire, Water, and Earth. In general, most Wiccan, Pagan, and metaphysical philosophies consider these elements to be symbolic representations of the potential energy that radiates from deity, as well as from various archetypal sources.

Philosophically and symbolically, the four elements remain the primary focus of power and energy in most magickal religious systems. These elements are believed to be universal principles, which, when understood, controlled, and arranged in a certain way, help the individual devise a more perfect reality.

As a nature based religion, Wicca tends to endorse the importance (and employment) of the four elements in its teachings and magickal rites. The energy contained in each of the four elements affects the way we think, feel, and behave; it is indispensable to the creative processes. The understanding of nature, environment, and self is a prerequisite to the understanding of spirit and deity.

Learning about the elements and the areas of your life they control is an important step in your spiritual development. Once you begin to harmonize with these magical forces of nature, you become aware of their knowledge and wisdom. The insight you gain from interacting with the elements will help balance your thinking and emotions. This balance is important because a spiritual focus is difficult if you are overwhelmed with passion, inflamed with anger, or given to flights of fancy.

Almost everything we come in contact with is associated with the elements. The elements correspond to the seasons, different times of the day and night, and even to plants, stones, and places. Astrologically, the elements provide the data for understanding different personality types and modes of expression. Without a doubt, the elements are one of nature's greatest contributions. They are a wondrous storehouse of knowledge just waiting to be explored.

The Element of Air

 Air is the subtle material realm between the physical and spiritual planes. Air speaks to the intellect and brings forth the true essence of the individual through the creative imagination. The element of air represents new beginnings, the thought process, and creativity.

Air has always been associated with breath, which is synonymous with the spirit or soul of all living creatures. The idea of air or breath giving life to the soul or spirit dates back to the time of matriarchal rule. After giving birth, mothers would gently breathe into their children's mouths, initiating the breathing process. In Greece, the female air soul was Pneuma, or the Muse, who always brought inspiration, giving poets and seers the power of understanding.

Breathing is fundamental to life. Breath enters our bodies at birth and leaves at death. Many have believed that the soul or spirit leaves the body at death on the person's breath. For this reason, in the past, mirrors were held close to the mouth of a dying person in hopes of capturing his or her soul in the mirror. This belief was echoed in folklore that viewed mirrors as soul traps and the realm of the dead as the Hall of Mirrors.

Spiritually, Air comes from the East on the wings of the Archangel Raphael, whose name means Healer of God. One of this magnificent creature's abilities is to heal the physical body as well as the spirit. Raphael is usually depicted with a bow and arrow and a crystal vial of healing balm.

Air Correspondences

The following items are all associated with the element of Air. Use them collectively or separately to help create the proper, magickal atmosphere for working with Air. For example; a blue candle, an amethyst, and lavender incense placed next to your computer will greatly enhance the thinking process.

COLOR	Blue, silver, white, and gray
SYMBOLS	Circle, bird, bell, sylph, flute, chimes, clouds
TOOLS	Wand, rod, staff
PLANTS	Almond, broom, clover, eyebright, lavender, pine
STONES	Amethyst, sapphire, citrine, azurite
PLACES	Sky, mountaintops, tree tops, bluffs, airplanes
ZODIAC	Aquarius, Gemini, Libra
TIME	Spring, dawn
ARCHANGEL	Raphael
DIRECTION	East
PROCESS	Thinking, reading, speaking, praying, singing

The Element of Fire

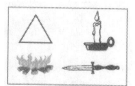

Fire is transformation; it is the life-giving generative powers of the sun. Fire is emblematic of the masculine deity in many cultures and is the element of fervent intensity, aspiration, and personal power. Fire is the force that motivates and drives all living organisms. Fire, along with air, creates energy, gets us going, and produces stamina. It has been said what the mind can imagine (Air), the will (Fire) can create.

Fire Correspondences

The following items are all associated with the element of Fire. Use them collectively or separately to help create the proper magickal atmosphere for working with the element of Fire. For example; meditating on the Archangel Michael and then placing a red candle next to his picture will help one gain personal energy and power.

COLOR	Red, red-orange (like flames), amber
SYMBOLS	Triangle, lightening, flame, salamander
TOOLS	Sword, dagger, fire pot, double-headed ax
PLANTS	Basil, dragon's blood, ginger, orange, tobacco
STONES	Ruby, garnet, diamond, bloodstone, flint, sunstone
PLACES	Volcanoes, ovens, fireplaces, deserts,
ZODIAC	Aries, Leo, Sagittarius
ARCHANGEL	Michael
TIME	Summer, noon
DIRECTION	South
PROCESS	Passion, anger, quick, active, energy, power

Fire is bright, brilliant, and flamboyant. Unfortunately, it is neither stable nor logical. Fire leaps intuitively to grasp the moment with little regard for what is around it. Fire is reckless, seeking, and passionate; it knows only itself. Fire is unique because in order for it to create, it must first consume or destroy. For example, a forest fire burns, consumes, and destroys the trees and underbrush. In time, however, new plants will grow. Fire is the active element within us. Fire pushes toward the new by getting rid of the old.

To use Fire correctly, you must first contain it. When you contain Fire, you can direct its energy toward a desired purpose, such as heat and light. You can also direct it with the personal forces it dominates, such as passion, anger, and aggression. When you control these emotions and channel their energy in a positive way, they bring about beneficial reconstruction. When these feelings go unchecked, they bring destruction and create chaos—just like Fire itself.

The Archangel Michael, the supreme commander of the Armies of Light, spiritually brings us Fire. This illuminating agent of Divine Light, whose name means Perfect of God, is the guardian of the southern quadrant. He is visualized as a Roman soldier, dressed in red and gold and ready to do battle against evil.

The Element of Water

 Water is passive and receptive. It has long been seen as the source of all potentialities in existence, and is associated with the Great Mother, the universal womb, birth, and fertility. Water is emblematic of the universe's life-giving and life-destroying abilities. Water is used to cleanse or purify physically as well as psychically.

Whereas Air is the intellect and Fire the energy or drive, Water is the emotional response to situations. Fluid, responsive, and giving, Water is sensitivity and emotion. Water is like the Great Mother and, when heated by the Fire God's passion, brings forth life. When it is cooled by the midnight air, silence and death are imminent. Many religions use immersion in water to symbolize the return to a primordial

---

Water Correspondences

The following items are all associated with the element of Water. Use them collectively or separately to help create the proper magickal atmosphere for working with Water. For example; put a moonstone in a chalice filled with water. Place the chalice in a window where the light of the full moon can shine on it all night. Drink the water to increase psychic abilities.

COLOR	Green, turquoise
SYMBOLS	Crescent, shells, boats, ship's wheel, anchor, cup
TOOLS	Vessel, grail, chalice, cauldron
PLANTS	Aloe, cucumber, dulse, gardenia, lily, lotus, willow
STONES	Aquamarine, moonstone, mother-of-pearl
PLACES	Oceans, rivers, lakes, ponds, waterfalls, beaches
ZODIAC	Cancer, Scorpio, Pisces
ARCHANGEL	Gabriel
TIME	Autumn, sunset
DIRECTION	West
PROCESS	Love, nurture, sensitivity, psychic ability, healing

state of purity. In essence, the baptism or dunking of an individual in water signifies the death and rebirth of the body and spirit.

The element of Water is both detached and willful when it flows freely. However, there are times when Water will allow itself to be contained. Water is a gentle element, and it inspires intuition and the desire to worship. The element of Water is linked to and part of the Goddess within all of us. Water is remembering the past and foreseeing the future. But as Water brings life, it can also bring destruction; the key lies in governing its energy.

Gabriel is the Archangel of the West, and the spiritual aspect of Water. He is destined to sound the last trumpet. Gabriel, like Water, symbolizes fertility in all its forms. His role is that of an initiator, and he is pictured holding the Grail as he emerges from the sea of immortality in the West.

The Element of Earth

 The Earth is solid, passive in nature, and negative in polarity. The Earth symbolically represents both the womb and the grave; that which brings life forth and that which takes away or reclaims it. However, unlike Water, the Earth is stationary and does not actively create. The Earth is seen mystically as the final outcome. It provides the other three elements with a place to physically manifest a desire. Earth is our base of operation and where we exhibit the final product of our imagination.

Earth is related to the flesh and all physical matter. It holds, nourishes, and affirms. Earth sees, touches, smells, senses, and feels; it is both sensual and practical. It can be stubborn as well as generous, and has instincts rather than feelings for the cycles and seasons of time. Earth is slow and steady, ever-changing yet always the same.

Auriel is the Archangel for the element of Earth. He brings the awareness of the gods as manifested in the beauty of creation, so that as we behold the wonders of nature, we are driven to consider the even greater splendor of the forces that created it. This Archangel operates at levels beyond that

Earth Correspondences

The following items are all associated with the element of Earth. Use them collectively or separately to help create the proper magickal atmosphere for working with Earth. For example, wear a moss agate and some patchouli oil to become more responsible.

SYMBOLS	Square, cornucopia, spindle, scythe, salt
TOOLS	Shield, pentacle, flail, horn
PLANTS	Alfalfa, cotton, oats, patchouli, vetivert, wheat
STONES	Moss agate, jasper, malachite, peridot, tourmaline
PLACES	Caves, forests, fields, gardens, canyons
ZODIAC	Capricorn, Taurus, Virgo
ARCHANGEL	Auriel
TIME	Midnight, winter
DIRECTION	North
PROCESS	Grounded, practical, organized, steady, responsible

of physical sight and teaches a sense of cosmic rightness. Auriel bears a glowing lantern in his left hand and a pair of scales in his right.

Wicca, like all magickal-religious systems, relies on nature and natural symbolism to create a connection between the conscious and unconsciousness minds. Without effort, the elements and their associated symbols elevate an individual's consciousness to a realm of higher understanding and awareness. Thus elemental symbolism helps to direct our energy toward a desired goal by using the elements' own natural magick.

Chapter 7

Sacred Wiccan Symbols

"The symbol expresses or crystallizes some aspect or direct experience of life and truth, and thus leads beyond itself."
—J. C. Cooper, *Traditional Symbols*

I n the Wiccan religion, symbols are considered to be instruments of knowledge. They reveal those aspects of reality that escape other modes of expression. Symbols impart a greater understanding of universal truths than mere words can convey.

Silently, yet profoundly, symbols speak to the spirit, intellect, and emotions, creating an everlasting impression. It is through the integration of symbols and abstract concepts that we tap into the cosmic consciousness. This awareness of the universe brings us into alignment with both deity and our own divine sparks.

Symbols surround us and speak to our minds without words. The red, octagonal sign at the end of the road tells us to stop; the cross at the top of a peaked roof tells us the building is a Christian church; a pentagram hanging around someone's neck indicates his or her spiritual beliefs.

Symbols represent actions and desires and allow us to tap into our higher self. They help us connect to that which they represent. In turn, the energy we force through this connection affects what resides at the opposite end. A good example would be blowing air through a straw. Whatever is in the path of the air flow will be forced to move. Energy always affects or changes that which it comes in contact with.

The four major symbols of Wicca are the wand, the dagger, the chalice, and the pentacle. These symbols represent the four elemental powers of nature: Air, the realm of wind and elemental sylphs; Fire, the realm of lightning and salamanders; Water, the realm of sea and undines; Earth, the realm of stone and gnomes. Just as the four elemental powers help us to control our physical lives, their symbolic representations aid us in our magickal and ritual work.

The Wand

The wand is ideally suited for directing personal power. Its phallic, tubular shape allows intellectual psychic energy to be channeled toward a desire objective. By virtue of its shape alone, it is masculine in nature. During ritual, the wand becomes an extension of the individual using it. Personal power is forced with a laser-like intensity toward the desired goal. The wand is the tool of creation; through it the seeds of desire are allowed to manifest. In all of magick, myth, and legend, wands have always been able to make wishes come true.

In Witchcraft, the wand is associated with Air (intellect), and East (new beginnings). The wand is usually made from a young tree branch of willow, rowan, or oak. It measures in length from the tip of the middle finger to the inside of the elbow. The directional end of the wand is usually fitted with a crystal or small pine cone, or is carved into a phallic shape. Leather cord, silver or copper wire, and feathers can be added for decoration.

The Athame

In most Wiccan traditions, the athame represents Fire and the masculine/ positive force of nature. There is good reason for this. Think about the process used to create a knife. Before the technology of iron smelting, knives were fashioned from flint. When the flint was rubbed with another piece of flint, it would produce a spark. Whether the knife was fashioned by hand with flint or forged into shape from an iron smelting process, the element of fire was involved, leaving an indelible impression of its essential masculine quality within the blade.

Traditionally, the athame is a small double-edged dagger. It measures about nine inches in length and has a black handle. The athame is considered to be an extension of one's magickal strength and power. It can be used for casting the magick circle, directing energy, or for banishing negative spirits.

The Chalice

 Ocean tides and the fluid, watery realms of our beginnings push and pull us into sympathetic response with our surroundings. This feminine reverberation, an emotional union with nature, causes us to react. Properly embraced, emotions keep us in balance, but unbridled passion will create havoc and dissipate energy.

The chalice is receptive and feminine in nature. It is restrictive and controlling because it contains the hidden mystery of life. By design it is emblematic of the womb, the Mother Goddess, and the ability to regenerate.

In most Wiccan traditions, the chalice represents mystery, hope, and promise. It is open to observation, while only the surface of what it contains can be seen. One must delve deeply within to discover its secrets.

The Pentacle

 The Pentacle is not so much a tool as it is the representation of the practitioner's ability to create or manifest desire. Witches use the pentacle to conceptualize their thoughts, believing that what they see in their mind's eye they will surely realize in physical form. During ritual, the pentacle becomes the point of focus where all energy is directed. Items such as amulets, charms, and talismans are placed on the pentacle for blessing or charging.

The pentacle is a flat stone or a wood or metal disk. It is associated with the North, the element of Earth, and the concept of reward. The beauty of the pentacle is its versatility. It provides the practitioner of magick with a mode of expression, like the canvas of an artist. You can place any number of unique symbols or designs on its face to represent your higher magical ideal.

Symbols, and tools are the visual aids that enhance and accentuate the different aspects of spiritual work. Whether you are meditating, praying, or performing a special ritual, these objects create atmosphere, aid in concentration, and focus energy. Religious symbols are links to deity and make

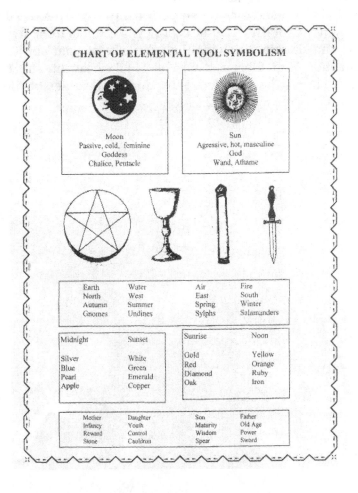

CHART OF ELEMENTAL TOOL SYMBOLISM

Moon
Passive, cold, feminine
Goddess
Chalice, Pentacle

Sun
Agressive, hot, masculine
God
Wand, Athame

Earth	Water	Air	Fire
North	West	East	South
Autumn	Summer	Spring	Winter
Gnomes	Undines	Sylphs	Salamanders

Midnight	Sunset	Sunrise	Noon
Silver	White	Gold	Yellow
Blue	Green	Red	Orange
Pearl	Emerald	Diamond	Ruby
Apple	Copper	Oak	Iron

Mother	Daughter	Son	Father
Infancy	Youth	Maturity	Old Age
Reward	Control	Wisdom	Power
Stone	Cauldron	Spear	Sword

contact and changes of consciousness very easy to accomplish; this is why they have been used throughout the centuries.

For personal reflection, the most significant expressions of deity are the Chalice and Athame. With proper use they become more than just symbols—they represent your ability to control and direct your personal power. They are the repositories of the dynamic energy you channel from divinity, and therefore provide the substance of your spiritual intention. With them you can travel to the heavenly spheres and retrieve the knowledge, wisdom, and understanding available only to those of vision.

Chapter 8

The Wiccan Temple

"Casting the circle is an enacted meditation. Each gesture we make, each tool we use, each power we invoke, resonates through layers of meaning to awaken an aspect of ourselves."
—Starhawk, *The Spiral Dance*

T he Wiccan temple, considered sacred space, is an area or room set aside for the reverence and worship of a deity. Once created, the personal temple radiates the glory and sovereignty of the god or goddess whose house it has become. In time, just like the great cathedrals, the temple area becomes filled with energy — one only needs to come within range of the area to feel the power, hope, and intent projected by its resident god or goddess.

The personal temple is considered to be a physical model of the universe, whose psychic energy it represents. It sets the standard for inner and outer spiritual organization and exhibits an understanding of the cosmology of the natural world. Everything contained within the Wiccan temple has meaning and purpose. The Wiccan temple holds the power and potential to evoke the elusive quality of the spirit, which is manifested when contact with a deity is made.

The Sacred Circle

Most Wiccan temples contain a circle, which defines the sacred working space. When actively consecrated, this physical border becomes a boundary between the human world and the realm of the Mighty Ones. Symbolically, the circle represents celestial unity, cyclic movement, and completion. The circle is feminine in nature and serves to contain, as does the womb, all life and energy raised within it. The circle is an important feature of most Pagan religions because it can be created anywhere, and provides a symbolic ring of protection where a deity can be invoked.

The Altar

The most important part of the Wiccan temple and circle is the altar, the point of focus where all obeisance is directed during ritual. The altar is sacred because it reflects the potential and power of the deity. In a sense, the altar is a repository for divine energy and an extension of the devotee's mind that allows for the acquisition of spiritual wisdom during worship. The altar serves to join the spiritual and material realms and as such is where human and deities meet.

The altar is usually placed within the center of the circle, making it the point of focus for all participants. The altar is covered with a cloth, on top of which are placed two candles (one to the right and one to the left) to represent the masculine and feminine powers of nature. The pentacle is placed in the center of the altar, with a candle on top of it. This candle is usually colored according to the seasonal rite. For example, there will be a green candle for Beltane and a black one for Samhain. Next to the pentacle are two small bowls, one filled with salt and one filled with water. The chalice is placed to the left of the pentacle and is usually filled with wine. The athame is then placed to the right of pentacle, along with the censer for burning incense.

On the floor, around the altar, a circle is inscribed to create a physical boundary for the magickal rite. At each of the four cardinal points, an appropriate colored candle is placed to represent the quadrant element. A blue candle is placed in the east, a red one in the south, a green one in the west and a yellow one in the north.

Creating Sacred Space

Once the physical boundaries of a temple have been set, the area will be prepared spiritually. The act of preparing an area for ritual work is called creating sacred space, and it is an essential part of all Wiccan ceremonies. The act of creating sacred space takes the form of casting or constructing a magick circle — an invisible psychic barrier. This is done in order to create the proper environment for spiritual and magickal rites. When the magick circle has been created, it will protect the individuals within its boundary from outside negative influence. The circle also serves to contain the energy raised within it until the time of release.

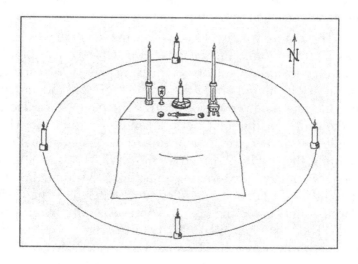

The casting of the magick circle is accomplished in two parts: the consecration of the elements (salt and water), and the psychic projection of energy onto the marked circle line. These two actions produce a sacred space and proper atmosphere for a ritual. It is important to understand that as you project the energy onto the physical circle line, you are in reality creating a sphere of total enclosure, rather than just a flat line of energy. When the casting is properly completed, you will feel as though you are inside a large ball of protective light.

Consecration of Salt and Water

The practitioner dips the tip of the athame into the water, saying:

> *Creature of water, cast out from thyself all impurities and uncleanliness of this world.*

The practitioner then dips the athame into the salt, saying:

Creature of earth, let only good enter to aid me in my work. So Mote It Be!

Casting the Sacred Circle

Three scoops of salt are stirred into the water, as the practitioner visualizes all negative thoughts and vibrations dissipating. Next, the practitioner will point the athame at the physical circle boundary. As the practitioner walks around the circle he or she will visualize a beam of energy or light flowing from the end of the athame onto the circle boundary, as he or she says:

I conjure and create thee, O circle of power, that shall be a boundary between the world of men and the realm of the mighty ones. A sphere of protection that shall preserve and contain all powers raised within. I now bless and consecrate thee O circle of power, to be a place of peace love and power. So Mote It Be!

Calling in the Guardians

Once the circle has been cast, the protective Guardians of the circle are called in. Guardians are highly evolved soul-minds who are attached or attracted to humans and the earth vibration. They can be Archangels or Higher Energy Forces in alignment with archetypal elemental forms. The calling in of the Guardians places these energy forces on the exterior of the circle for added power and protection.

The practitioner will begin by pointing the athame at the eastern quadrant, visualizing the Guardian approaching, as if from a distance, up to the boundary of the circle.

As this is done, the practitioner will evoke the Guardians, saying:

East

Hear me O Mighty One, Ruler of the Whirlwinds,
Guardian of the Eastern Portal,
I do summon and call thee forth, bear witness to these
rites, as you shield and protect
this gateway between the worlds.

South

Hear me O Mighty One, Ruler of the Solar Orb,
Guardian of the Southern Portal,
I do summon and call thee forth, bear witness to these
rites, as you shield and protect
this gateway between the worlds.

West

Hear me O Mighty One, Ruler of the Mysterious
Depths, Guardian of the Western Portal,
I do summon and call thee forth, bear witness to these
rites, as you shield and protect
this gateway between the worlds.

North

Hear me O Mighty One, Ruler of the Forest and Field,
Guardian of the Northern Portal,
I do summon and call thee forth, bear witness to these
rites, as you shield and protect
this gateway between the worlds.

Once the circle has been cast and the Guardians called in, the area is ready for spiritual work. Generally, there are three kinds of spiritual work that require the protection of a consecrated circle. These include the eight Sabbat celebrations, magickal rites conducted during a full moon ritual, and rites of transition, such as initiation.

During the ritual, participants remain within the boundary of the circle until all activities come to an end. This prevents distraction and the dissipation of raised energy. When the main body of the ritual—for example, a Sabbat or full moon ceremony—has come to an end, the sacred space will be taken down.

Closing Sacred Space

Taking down or dismantling sacred space involves the same procedure as creating it—only everything is done in reverse. The Guardians of the four quadrants are dismissed, and then the circle is withdrawn. The practitioner will begin the dismissal in the north, pointing the athame at the northern quadrant while visualizing the Guardian returning to where it came from, and saying:

> *Hear me O mighty one, Ruler of Forest and Field,*
> *Guardian of the Northern Portal,*
> *I thank thee for thy blessings and protection, at this*
> *gateway between the worlds, and*
> *bid thee—hail and farewell.*

The practitioner continues dismissing the Guardians by moving widdershins (counterclockwise) around the circle, reciting, in the appropriate quadrant:

> *Hear me O Mighty One, Ruler of the Mysterious*
> *Depths, Guardian of the Western Portal,*
> *I thank thee for thy blessings and protection, at this*
> *gateway between the worlds, and*
> *bid thee—hail and farewell.*

Hear me O Mighty One, Ruler of the Solar, Guardian of the Southern Portal,
I thank thee for thy blessings and protection, at this gateway between the worlds, and
bid thee — hail and farewell.

Hear me O Mighty One, Ruler of the Whirlwinds, guardian of the Eastern Portal,
I thank thee for thy blessings and protection, at this gateway between the worlds, and
bid thee — hail and farewell.

Once the Guardians have been dismissed, the participant will "take up the circle," beginning in the north. He or she will point the athame at the circle boundary line and withdraw the psychic energy which was early placed there. As this is done, the participant says:

O Circle of power that has been a boundary between the world of men, and the realm of the Mighty Ones, that has served to preserve and contained all energy raised within, I now recall and withdraw your force of power. So Mote It Be.

The ritual has now come to an end. If the area in which the ritual took place is not a separate space, and is used for other activities, then the circle must be physically erased. The altar, tools, and all items used during the ritual should be put away. Only when an area has been set aside exclusively for ritual use are the altar and tools left in place.

Chapter 9

Fundamental Rites

"Ritual may be manmade in the sense that human hands fashioned it. But what inspired those hands to do their work is the Divine influence."
—Ben Zion Boksar,
Perspectives on a Troubled Decade

A ritual is a prescribed event or particular ceremony that is built up by tradition and carries a great amount of energy, light-force, and impact. It is a systematic procedure designed to achieve a particular effect on human consciousness. When repeated with the same intention, sacramental techniques, and working methods, ritual makes an impression—the results of which are the manifestation of desire.

Formalized ritual is the way most Wiccans approach divinity, align with the forces of nature, and celebrate seasonal cycles. Ritual is an important part of the Wiccan religion because it helps elevate the consciousness of the practitioner or group to a higher level of spiritual awareness.

For any ritual to have meaning, it must have Intention. This means there should be a reason for doing it, even if the reason is as simple as a thank you for a blessing received. The intention should be decided upon before the rite takes place and then adhered to. It is very difficult, if not impossible, to achieve results if motives and methods are constantly changing. The person conducting the ritual should know what to do and when to do it. When the details of a ritual have a purpose and are properly carried out, the energy flows and the connection with deity is made.

There are three reasons for doing a ritual. The first is alignment with divinity, elevating the spiritual focus or consciousness of the practitioner. The second is to celebrate a special day, time, or event, such as a Sabbat, full moon, or personal transition. The third is to create or manifest a goal through magic and spell-crafting.

Once the reason for the ritual has been determined, the ceremony is then constructed. All rituals have five separate, though related, segments. No single segment constitutes a ritual, but when they are combined they create a working spiritual arrangement.

The first segment of a formal Wiccan ritual is the Creation of Sacred Space, discussed in Chapter 8. When sacred space has been created, the practitioner will invite the God and/or Goddess into the space through prayer, or Invocation. Once the deity is present, the Intention, or reason for doing the rite, is expressed through some sort of physical action, such as a seasonal drama, an awe-inspiring dance, the rendering of a myth, or a guided meditation. Following the intention comes the Rite of Union, during which cakes and wine are blessed. The final segment of the ritual is the Closing, which brings the ritual to an end, and dismantles the sacred space.

Invocation

The invocation is usually in the form of a poetic verse or song that formally draws down the essence of the deity into the practitioner and sacred space. In most ritual settings, the practitioner faces the altar with arms raised as he or she speaks the invoking words. The idea is to merge human consciousness with that of the deity. When the connection is complete, the essence of the deity flows directly through the practitioner, permeates the area of ritual worship, and is used to enhance the ritual or magical rites being performed.

The Invocation of the Goddess

In a coven setting, the High Priestess usually invokes the Goddess near the beginning of the ritual. She will face the altar, take several relaxing breaths, and then, with great reverence, call upon the Goddess. (Note that Cerridwen is the Celtic mother goddess of grain, and that you may substitute the name of another goddess or god you are working with for this part of the invocation.)

Thou who whispers gentle yet strong
Thou for whom my soul doth long,
By most men you are seldom seen
Yet you ever reign, as virgin, mother, queen,
Through the veil you pass with pride
As I beckon thee now to be at my side,
Cerridwen!

Thou who knows, thou who conceals
Thou who gives birth, thou who feels,
For you are the goddess, and mother to all.
Pray thee now, come as I call,
Now through the mist, I hear your voice
And invoke thee most gracious goddess by choice,
Cerridwen!

Thou who suffers as all men die
Doth with her victim in love lie,
For you are the goddess, and crone of despair
To our ending with you, we must share,
I feel thy passion, and fell thy presence
I desire to be one with thy vital essence,
Cerridwen!

I pray thee dancer of eternal bliss
Bestow upon me thy wondrous kiss.
Let now thy light, love, and power
Descend, become one, with me this hour,
For you are the creatress of heaven and earth
To my soul and spirit you have given birth,
Cerridwen!

The Invocation of the God

The invocation of the God is usually performed by the High Priest. He will face the altar, as did the High Priestess, and call upon the God.

Father of death, father of night
Father of birth, father of light
Cernunnos, Cernunnos, Cernunnos

Come by Flame, Come by fire
Come now, whom we desire
Cernunnos, Cernunnos, Cernunnos

O Horned one, O ancient one
God of the sun, Bringer of light
The powers of Darkness put to flight.
O Horned one, O ancient one
Who comes from beyond the gates of death and birth
Come who gives life to all on earth

Come, I Invoke Thee
For you are Pan, Apollo, Cernunnos
Lord of Hades, Lord of death
You are them all, yet you are he.

Come, come my Lord, I beckon thee.
Come, come my lord, of wild delights
Come, join with us in these secret-mystic rites.
Come, come my lord, of fire and flame
As I call out your sacred and holy name
Cernunnos, Cernunnos, Cernunnos.

The Intention

The next step in the ritual procedure is that of the Intention: the reason for doing the ritual. During the Intention the main body of the ritual is developed. For example, seasonal celebrations will focus on time honored themes such as planning, planting, harvesting, and remembering. Full moon rituals will concentrate on lunar themes, the feminine aspect of deity, or magical operations.

This portion of the ritual is where individual creativity blossoms. The intention can be as simple or elaborate as the practitioner wishes. The solitary Witch will usually keep this portion of the ritual fairly simple, using a cherished poem or prayer to express his or her desires. The coven or large group might use this time for a guided meditation to present a drama based on a mystery teaching, or to participate in an activity like dancing around the Maypole. Whatever the activity is, it should be appropriate to the season and theme of the rite.

The Rite of Union

The Rite of Union, the blessing of bread and wine, is a common act in most Wiccan and Mystery traditions. During this segment of the rite, wine and bread (or cake) are blessed and then shared among members in honor of deity. In most ceremonies the wine is symbolic of the blood, or life essence, of the God, and the bread (or cake) the body or energy of the Goddess. When the wine and bread are consumed by the participants of the ritual, they are spiritually transformed through the divine symbolic attributes of the food.

Solitary Wiccans act out the Rite of Union as part of their rituals just as covens do. During the rite, the wine will be blessed, transforming it into the vital essence of the God. Once this process has been completed, the sacred fluid is poured into the chalice (the physical symbolic representation of the Goddess). The chalice is then conjoined with the athame (the physical symbolic representation of the God) to form the perfect union of masculine and feminine energy.

How to Perform the Rite of Union (wine)

The couple performing the Rite of Union will need a chalice, athame, and two containers of wine, one red and one white (red and white grape juice may be used as a substitute). One is filled with white wine, and the other with red wine.

The Rite of Union is most often performed by the leaders of the Coven, the priest and priestess. At the appropriate time, they approach the altar and genuflect or bow. The priest, or lead male LM, picks up the chalice, and the priestess, or lead female LF, picks up the containers of wine, one

Lead Female (Priestess) pouring the wine into the chalice held by the Lead Male (Priest).

white and one red. They then turn and face each other. She holds the wine as pictured and he kneels facing her, holding the chalice.

LF pours the red and white wine into the chalice, combining them as she says the following:

I pour the red and the white, that they shall mix, as life and death, joy and sorrow,
peace, and humility, and impart their essence of wonder unto all.

LM remains kneeling as he holds the chalice filled with the wine, saying:

*For I am the father, lover, and brother unto all. The
bringer of life, and the giver of death
before whom all time is ashamed. Let my spirit breathe
upon you and awaken the fires of
inspiration within your soul.*

LF replaces the containers of wine on the altar and picks
up the athame. She slowly lowers it into the chalice as LM
rises with the chalice to meet the blade of the athame so it
touches the wine within. While doing this, they say:

LF: *For as this athame represents the male, and the God.*

LM: *And this chalice represents the female, and the
Goddess.*

Both: *They are conjoined to become one, in truth, power,
and wisdom.*
So Mote It Be.

LF replaces the athame upon the altar. LM takes a sip
of the wine, hands it to LF, and says:

"Perfect love and perfect trust."

LF takes a sip and passes it back to LM, saying:

"Perfect love and perfect trust."

The chalice is passed to each member of the group, who
respond in turn:

"Perfect love and perfect trust."

How to Perform the Rite of Union (bread)

Blessing bread takes on the same significance as does
the blessing of wine. During the blessing, the vital essence

of the Goddess is drawn down into bread or cake, making it sacred.

The act of blessing the bread will again be done by the lead female of the group and the lead male. The bread will have been placed on a plate or on the pentacle before the ritual. (Small biscuits or common bread purchased from religious supply houses work best as they are small and made especially for religious rites.) As the Rite of Union comes to a close, LF and LM prepare to begin the blessing of the sacramental bread.

LF picks up the plate of bread and faces LM, saying:

Behold the sovereignty of our Divine King
Beloved son and lover
Radiant and everlasting light
Guardian of the souls of man who rises triumphant
from the tomb.

LM responds by saying:

We give honor to thee, O sacrificed God
Who through the Mother grants eternity.
By shedding your blood upon the land,
All are transformed through your passion
As they pass through the gates of judgment.

He picks up a piece of bread, holds it over the plate, and recites in unison with LF:

Let now the mystery be revealed
Of the light of the Lord within,
Who in the shadow of the Goddess
Will ever reign supreme.
So Mote It Be!

As with the wine, the bread is passed among the members so each may receive a portion of the god's blessing.

How to Perform the Solitary Rite of Union (wine)

This is a simplified version of the actual Rite of Union and can be used by those who practice and worship alone. The practitioner will fill the chalice with red and white wine before the ritual. When the time comes to perform the Rite of Union, the practitioner will face the altar, genuflect or bow, and pick up the chalice. While holding the chalice in offering, the practitioner will say the following as he or she visualizes the energy of the God and Goddess flowing into the chalice:

My Lord is the power and force of all life,
My Lady is the vessel through which all life flows.
My Lord is life and death,
My Lady is birth and renewal.
The sun brings forth life,
The moon holds it in darkness.

The practitioner will then place the chalice on the altar. He or she will pick up the athame, plunge it into the chalice and say:

For as the lance is to the male,
So the grail is to the female,
And together they are conjoined to become one
In truth, power, and wisdom.

The practitioner then takes a sip of the wine in honor of his or her god and goddess.

How to Perform the Solitary Rite of Union (bread)

Before the ritual, the practitioner will place the bread or cake on a small plate or on top of the pentacle. As soon as the wine has been blessed, the practitioner will bless the bread by holding his or her hands over the bread and speaking:

O Great Lord of Heavenly power
Whose presence reigns from above
Be with me in this ritual hour
And grace this bread with your love.
So Mote It Be!

The Full Moon

The moon has always been associated with the Goddess, Witchcraft, and the occult side of nature. In many cultures, the Moon Goddess and the Creatress were one and the same. Ancient Egypt identified Isis and Hathor with the crescent moon. The Phoenicians called their goddess Astarte the Queen of Heaven with Crescent Horns. The Greek goddess Artemis, lover of the woods and the wild chase, was symbolized by the moon. The Romans named their moon goddesses Diana, Luna, Herodias, and Lucina, who governed the tides. Later, the mysterious Hecate joined the pantheon, and was known as the Goddess of the Dark of the Moon.

During the Middle Ages, occult philosophers believed the moon to be alchemical silver and the sun alchemical gold. Those who worked magic of any kind observed the movement of the moon. Witches invoked the Goddess by drawing down the moon, a rite dating back to centuries before the Christian era.

There are 13 full moons in the Wiccan calendar, and each is related to the season in which it falls. The naming of the full moons was started during the early centuries of the Christian era as an aid in farming and animal husbandry. This is why most of the designations reflect natural phenomena and the importance of hunting and agriculture. Even though most of us do not hunt or farm, the subtle implication of the energy present at each full moon can be focused for spiritual or intellectual endeavors.

Full Moon Names

November (*Snow Moon*): Scorpio brings in the dark season and Winter begins. This is the death of the season, a time to dispose of the dead wood of the year and analyze what is healthy and unhealthy within our lives.

December (*Oak Moon*): The mighty oak withstands the cold hardship of winter. The oak is revered for its longevity and the fact that such a mighty creature comes from the smallest acorn. Now is the time to remain steadfast in convictions and principles as plans are made for the coming year.

January (*Wolf Moon*): The wolf is a fearsome creature of the night and a companion to the Witch and Shaman. The wolf protects and guards his home and family. This is a time to protect what we have as we consider new options.

February (*Storm Moon*): A storm is said to rage most fiercely just before it ends, and the year usually follows suit. The end of winter, death, and darkness is coming. It is time to plan for the future and what we will pursue in the months to come.

March (*Chaste Moon*): All is new, fresh, and virginal as life begins anew. The antiquated word for pure reflects the custom of greeting the new year with a clear consciousness. Now we can begin to plant the seeds of desire.

April (*Seed Moon*): Spring is in the air. This is the time of sowing seeds (spiritual or physical), the time when we physically put our desires into motion.

May (*Hare Moon*): The sacred animal was associated in Roman legends with springtime and fertility. All life is blossoming forth. Now is the time we use the creative spirit to reaffirm our goals.

June (*Dyad Moon*): Dyad is the Latin name for pair, the twin stars of Castor and Pollux. This is a time of equality, union of opposites, and duality. It is the time to seek balance between our spiritual and physical desires.

July *(Mead Moon)*: Mead was the traditional beverage in old Europe. This was a time for working to preserve some of those crops (mostly for wine- and ale-making) for winter and future use. It is the time to plan for what we will do when we reach our goals.

August *(Wort Moon)*: Wort is the Anglo-Saxon term for herb or green plant. This is the first harvest and a time to celebrate. It is a good time to plan for preserving what we have attained.

September *(Barley Moon)*: We enter the sign of Virgo, the virgin who carries sheaves of barely and grain. This is the great harvest, a time for celebration and the realization of desired goals.

October *(Blood Moon)*: This moon marks the season of hunting and the slaughter of the animals for winter food and clothing. Blood is the force of life. Now is the time for thanksgiving, rest, and reflection.

Blue Moon *(Variable)*: This occurs when the full moon appears twice within the same calendar month. A blue moon is considered to be extremely lucky and is used for magical rites that are in alignment with luck, prosperity, and good fortune.

Celebrating the Full Moon

The moon is more than just the sun's reflected glory; it is the majestic personification of the past, present, and future. Even our ancestors noted how the moon's waxing and waning corresponded to the sea tides and the behavior patterns of people, animals, and plants. To the modern Witch, the moon is the mistress of all magic, and a symbol of the Goddess, who rules the night sky, the earth, and all in the land of spirits beneath it.

The full moon is a time of immense — and intense — psychic power. When there is a difficult task at hand, the Witch will use the full moon to resolve it. This is why magical activities are planned to coincide with rising of the full moon. The Witch knows it is in his or her best interest to take advantage of the moon's power when it is at its peak. Any good astrological calendar will provide you with the date and time of the full moon. It will also be listed in the *Old Farmer's Almanac*, which you'll find in almost any book or grocery store.

A Full Moon Ritual for Solitary Practice

Items Needed:

▶ Two white altar candles.

▶ One silver pillar candle to represent the Goddess.

▶ Athame or wand.

▶ Chalice.

▶ Pentacle.

▶ Incense burner and incense.

▶ Wine or fruit juice.

1. Consecrate the elements, cast the circle, and call in the Guardians.

2. Light the two white altar candles. Begin with the right one, as you say:

Right Candle

Lunar mistress meek and mild
    Look upon your seeking child,
With this candle I now light
    Please bring me joy on this night.

Left Candle

> *I now approach thee of gentle grace*
> > *To bless and protect this sacred space,*
> *With this torch of truth and praise*
> > *Guide me through my nights and days.*
> *So Mote It Be!*

3. Pick up the censer, add incense, and walk to the East. Hold the incense in offering as you say:

> *I offer the element of Air, for insight and wisdom.*

Return the censer to the altar, pick up the right candle, and proceed to the South. Hold the candle in offering as you say:

> *I offer the element of Fire, for strength and power.*

Return the candle to the altar, pick up the water bowl, and go to the West. Hold the bowl in offering as you say:

> *I offer the element of Water, for control and dominion.*

Return the bowl to the altar, pick up the salt bowl, and go to the North. Hold the bowl in offering as you say:

> *I offer the element of Earth, for the manifestation of desire.*

4. Return the bowl of salt to the altar. Light the Goddess's silver pillar candle as you recite the following prayer:

> *Mistress of magic, lady of the night,*
> > *mother of mist, moor, and moonlight.*
> *Great indeed is your awesome power,*
> > *Which illuminates my world this hour.*
> *I ask you keep my heart — happy and free,*
> > *And bless me with love, health and prosperity.*
> *For this I will, so let it be!*

5. Remain facing the altar and invoke the Goddess:

Thou who whispers gentle yet strong
Thou for whom my soul doth long,
By most men you are seldom seen
Yet you ever reign, as virgin, mother, queen.
Through the veil you pass with pride
As I beckon thee now to be at my side,
Cerridwen!

Thou who knows, thou who conceals,
Thou who gives birth, thou who feels,
For you are the Goddess, and mother to all
Pray thee now, come as I call,
Now through the mist, I hear your voice
And invoke thee most gracious goddess by choice,
Cerridwen!

Thou who suffers as all men die
Doth with her victim in love lie,
For you are the Goddess and crone of despair
To our ending with you, we must share.
I feel thy passion, and feel thy presence
I desire to be one with thy vital essence,
Cerridwen!

I pray thee dancer of eternal bliss,
Bestow upon me thy wondrous kiss
Let now thy light, love, and power
Descend, become one, with me this hour,
For you are the creatress of heaven and earth
To my soul and spirit you have given birth,
Cerridwen!

6. After the invocation, the intention of the ritual is expressed. This is where your personal input and energy will make the

ritual unique. Use this time to focus your attention on magick, meditation, or spiritual healing.

7. When you have completed your ritual work, you will want to perform the solitary *Rite of Union*. Pick up the chalice and hold it in offering as you say the following:

> *My Lord is the power and force of all life,*
> *My Lady is the vessel through which all life flows.*
> *My Lord is life and death,*
> *My Lady is birth and renewal.*
> *The Sun brings forth life,*
> *The Moon holds it in darkness.*

Place the chalice back on the altar. Pick up the athame and plunge it into the chalice as you say:

> *For as the Lance is to the male,*
> *So the Grail is to the female,*
> *And together they are conjoined to become one*
> *In truth, power, and wisdom.*

8. Begin the closing of your ceremony by extinguishing the altar candles. Start with the left one:

Left

> *Let now the power, potential, and force*
> *Return unto the original source.*

Right

> *Let now the motion, direction, and sight*
> *Return unto the original light.*

9. Dismiss the Guardians and take up the circle.

A Full Moon Ritual for Three or More

There are advantages to working and worshiping with others of like mind. For one thing, everyone shares in setting up, ritual participation, and closing. Another benefit of group ritual is the ability to raise and channel great amounts of energy toward magickal endeavors. In addition, there is the personal bonding that takes place when people share spiritual activities.

The following ritual is designed for at least three people, with the ideal being six or more. Two people will be chosen as the leaders and there will need to be two to four attendants. All of the speaking parts are labeled LM, LF, or ATT (for attendant).

When working with other people in a group setting, it is best to have copies of the ritual for everyone, especially for those people who have speaking parts. Always take a few moments before starting the ritual to go over individual speaking parts and activities. When people know what is expected of them, the ritual runs smoothly and everyone has a good time.

For this full moon ceremony, the altar is covered with a white cloth. On it are placed the two main altar candles (near the back, one to the left and one to the right), the chalice filled with white wine (on the left side of the altar, in front of the left candle), the athame (on the right side of the altar in front of the right candle): the salt and water bowls (front and center), and the censer (to the right of the bowls). In addition, there should be a bowl filled with spring water, fresh flowers, and a floating candle set in the center of the altar as a symbol of the Goddess.

1. ATT lights the altar candles, first the right one and then the left one, as he or she says:

> *Gentle mother meek and mild*
> *Look upon your seeking child,*
> *With this candle I now light*
> *Please bring us joy on this night.*
>
> *I approach you lady of gentle grace*
> *To bless and protect this sacred space,*
> *With this torch of truth and praise*
> *Gently guide us through all our days.*
> *So Mote It Be!*

2. LF consecrates the elements and casts the circle. LM calls in the Guardians of the four quadrants.

3. ATT offers the elements at each of the four quadrants (East-censer, South-altar candle, West-water, North-salt). He or she picks up the censer, walks to the East, and holds it in offering, saying:

> *There is but one spirit and it dwells within*
> *For it is the truth from where we begin.*

4. ATT returns the censer to the altar, picks up the candle, walks to the South, and holds it in offering, saying:

> *There is but one spark and it burns us like fire*
> *It comes from a passion brought forth from desire.*

5. ATT returns the candle to the altar, picks up the water bowl, walks to the West, and holds it in offering, saying:

> *There is but one feeling and it is our emotion*
> *It swells deep within, crashes forth like the ocean.*

6. ATT returns the candle to the altar, picks up the water bowl, walks to the West, and holds it in offering, saying:

> *There is but one reason and it comes from rebirth*
> *To live, love, and die with wisdom on Earth.*

7. ATT returns to the altar. He or she leads the group in the following proclamation, in unison:

> *There is but one spirit and it dwells within*
> *For it is the truth from where we begin.*
> *There is but one spark and it burns us like fire*
> *It comes from a passion brought forth from desire.*
> *There is but one feeling and it is our emotion*
> *It swells deep within and crashes forth like the ocean*
> *There is but one reason and it comes from rebirth*
> *To live, love, and die with wisdom on Earth.*

> *Ayea, ayea, Cerridwen*
> *Ayea, ayea, Cerridwen*
> *Ayea, ayea, Cerridwen*
> *Ayea, ayea, ayea.*

8. ATT approaches the altar and lights the floating candle. He or she holds the bowl in offering and recites the following:

> *Lady of desire, reflection of light*
> *You are motion, direction, and our second sight.*
> *Mother of creation, the original source*
> *You are potential, power, the ultimate force.*
> *Grandmother of time, wise one from above,*
> *Do we summon thee here with honor and love.*

9. ATT hands the bowl to LM, who says:

> *Gracious Goddess and mother of all,*
> *Give us the wisdom to discover you,*
> *The intelligence to understand you,*
> *The diligence to seek after you,*
> *The patience to wait for you,*
> *The openness of mind to accept you,*
> *And the dedication to proclaim you.*
> *We welcome you within our hearts*
> *Now and forever, So Shall It Be!*

10. LM places the bowl back on the altar. He picks up the chalice and kneels facing LF. He holds the chalice in offering to her as he says the following:

> *Lady of the morning star*
> > *Queen of the heavenly sea*
> *Power of the mighty wind*
> > *You alone were chosen to be.*
>
> *Lady who guides the mighty angels*
> > *Mother of selfless devotion*
> *Enchantress of the mysteries*
> > *And keeper of time and motion.*
>
> *Lady we now invite thee here*
> > *As the virgin of pure love*
> *The one who moves the soul man*
> > *With her splendor from above.*
>
> *Lady we now invite thee here*
> > *As the mother of sacred Earth*
> *Whose power is beyond compare*
> > *When dreams are given birth.*

Lady we now invite thee here
  As the wisdom from the past
That within this holy grail
  Come blessings that will last.

11. LF places her hands over the chalice as she blesses the wine, saying:

Behold the brilliant evening star
  The virgin of celestial light
Behold the Goddess from afar
  The mother of second sight.

Behold the Queen of twilight hour
  The wise and vigilant protector
Behold the Goddess's silent power
  The mother most regal and splendor.

Behold the lady who must descend
  The mystery hidden beneath the veil
Behold the Goddess who rises again
  The keeper of the golden grail.

12. LF picks up the athame and, before plunging it into the chalice, exclaims:

I offer to thee courage and wisdom
  And I bring the strength and might
I offer to thee warmth and pleasure
  And I bring thee love and light.

I offer to thee the seed of the sun
  And I bring thee honor and power
I offer to thee the staff of life
  And I bring thee fruit and the flower.

13. LM hands the chalice to LF, who invokes the Goddess, as outlined earlier.

14. LF takes a sip of the wine. She hands it to LM, saying, *"perfect love and perfect trust."* He takes a sip of the wine and hands it to the person closest to him, saying, *"perfect love and perfect trust."* The wine is then passed around the circle, with each person taking a sip and saying *"perfect love and perfect trust."*

15. Beginning in the North, ATT says the following, and extinguishes the candle:

> *There is but one reason, it came from the Earth*
> *So to our dreams the gods would give birth.*

ATT walks to the West, says the following, and extinguishes the candle:

> *There is but one feeling, it comes from the ocean*
> *To help us learn control over each emotion.*

ATT walks to the South, says the following, and extinguishes the candle:

> *There is but one spark, it comes from fire*
> *Brings us the passion to create desire.*

ATT walks to the East, says the following, and extinguishes the candle:

> *There is but one spirit, it came from the air*
> *And with us its knowledge and wisdom did share.*

16. The first ATT will now extinguish the altar candles, first the left and then the right, as he or she says:

> *Let now the potential, power, and force*
> *Return unto the original source.*

Let now the motion, direction, and sight
Return unto the original light.

17. LM dismisses the Guardians and LF takes up the circle. The rite is now ended. Those members who served as attendants take down the altar and put all the items away.

Chapter 10

Seasons of Celebration

*"Seasonal rites are virtually as old as the hills
they used to be practiced on by most of humanity,
and even today they are kept up in very attenuated
forms by a small minority of cultists."*
—William G. Gray, *Seasonal Occult Rituals*

1 n Wicca, the natural year is measured by eight
major festivals, called Sabbats or Great Days.
These special times are the equinoxes, solstices, and
the four cross-quarter days that occur between them. Although most people are dimly aware of seasonal change,

Wiccans embrace the seasons with ardent enthusiasm. Festivals, both great and small, mark the beginning of winter, welcome the first breath of spring, proclaim the glory of summer, and revel in the harvest bounty.

The four major changes in the yearly cycle — winter, spring, summer, and fall — are divided into four minor, more subtle changes. For those who practice Wicca, these occasions are set aside to honor the God and Goddess, work magic, and give thanks for blessings received.

Sabbats occur approximately every six weeks. To those who practice Wicca, Sabbats are not just a change of season and weather, but rather are reflections of the life-cycle processes of birth, life, death, and rebirth. Physically as well as spiritually, we express our understanding of these principles by making use of these special times of power.

Using agriculture as our example, we view the seasons in terms of *planning, planting, harvesting,* and *resting.* In the early spring, the farmer will plan the garden, preparing to plant by late spring and early summer. In the late summer and early fall, the farmer will harvest the crops. In the late fall and winter all of nature rests and regenerates.

The Sabbats provide a natural time frame in which to work and measure personal progress. During the winter months, we think about what needs to be done or accomplished. In spring, we begin to prepare for the task at hand by formulating a plan of action and then planting the seeds of desire. During the summer months, we nurture and protect through hard work. With the coming of fall we are ready to harvest the fruits of our labors and receive the rewards for a job well done.

Many things go into making a Sabbat ritual work. Attention to proper symbolism, atmosphere, and ritual attire should be taken into consideration long before the event is to take place. Think of the Sabbat ceremony as a play you are performing for the God and Goddess. The more effort you put into the props and into your delivery of liturgy, the more influence your play will have. A properly performed ritual always makes an impression on the consciousness of those involved, as well as on the audience — be it human or divine.

One thing the solitary practitioner can do to make ritual special is to take the time to decorate. Use the standard altar arrangement described earlier. Then add seasonal decorations, flowers, ornaments, and freshly baked breads and cakes. Color coordinate candles, the altar cloth, and ribbons. If space permits, adorn the circle with flower petals, greenery, or brightly colored, braided ribbon.

Samhain: All Hallows' Eve

Samhain, which means "end of the summer," is celebrated on October 31. It is the end of the agricultural season and the beginning of the Celtic year. Samhain is the festival of the dead; it was Christianized when the day that follows it was designated All Souls' Day or All Saints' Day. This is a time of chaos and the reversal of normal order; endings and beginnings are occurring simultaneously.

For our ancestors, Samhain was when the majority of the herd was butchered, providing food for the winter months. Slaughter, barren earth, and decreasing daylight made the concept of death an ever present reality. Because of this, Samhain has always been considered a time when the veil between the worlds was thin, a night of magic charms and divination, when the dead could be easily contacted.

On an individual basis, this is the time to rest and re-evaluate your life and goals. Now is when you want to get rid of any negativity or opposition that may surround your achievements or hinder future progress. Samhain should have seen the accomplishment of your desires, and now you need to stabilize and protect what you have gained. This is important, since it is impossible to concentrate, let alone put energy into new goals, if what you have is not secure.

Ritual Tools, Symbols, and Decorations

Altar decorations: Black altar cloth, red altar candles, cauldron or pot with water and a floating candle, black pillar candle, bowl of apples, wand tied with black ribbon, lighted pumpkins, black silk pouch, chalice covered with a black cloth, red and white wine.

Plants and herbs: Acorn, oak, hazel, apple, fumitory, mullein, nightshade, pumpkin, sage, angelica, wormwood, mugwort, peppermint, bay, rosemary, sandalwood, ginger.

Oil: Mix rosemary and bay oils together for anointing, or use pure sandalwood oil.

Food: Roast beef, goose, duck, or turkey; apple fritters; apple pie; pumpkin pie; mashed turnips; baked acorn squash; mulled wine and cider; roasted potatoes and peppers; hazelnut cookies; peppermint tea; pumpkin bread; corn bread; corn relish; and red onion and beet salad.

Symbols: Jack-o-lanterns, cauldron, scrying mirror or bowl, tarot cards, torches, bonfires, graveyard, tombstone, broom, corn stalks, runes for casting, photographs of departed ancestors, oak and hazel wands tied with black ribbon.

For this special occasion, prepare a protection bag to bless during your ritual. Write your desire on a small square of paper and place it in a black silk or cotton bag along with stones for protection (onyx, black tourmaline, and obsidian), herbs for strength (bay, mulberry, and thistle), and something personal (a ring, a lock of hair, or a photograph).

A Ceremony for Samhain

Light the right altar candle and then the left one, as you say the following:

Right

> *Blessed be the dying King,*
> > *And the sacrifice of blood he shed.*
> *For he alone shall guide me,*
> > *Through the time of dark and dread.*

Left

> *Blessed be the Death Crone,*
> > *And her silent tides of death and birth.*
> *For she alone brings love,*
> > *Life and wisdom to this earth.*

At this point you will light each of the tea lights inside the four pumpkins. Pick up a pumpkin and place it in the East as you acknowledge the quadrant. Then place one in the South, the West, and the North, each time acknowledging the quadrant:

East

> *Let there be light in the East, the home of the eternal spirit.*

South

Let there be light in the South, the home of the divine spark.

West

Let there be light in the West, the home of rest and regeneration.

North

Let there be light in the North, the home of the final atonement.

Cast the circle, call in the Guardians. Face the altar, anoint the forehead with seasonal oil, and then speak the following:

Death brings life, life brings death.

Say the following blessing, and light the black pillar candle:

Let this flame radiate through the night
*   Bring forth great wisdom and much insight.*
At this sacred time, and in this holy place
*   I beckon those of the past to come and share my space.*

Pick up the bowl of apples. Hold the bowl in offering as you ask the following blessing:

The land has died, the earth is cold,
*   The Horned One comes from times of old.*
He brings the word, he is the Death,
*   He whispers my name with icy breath.*
Come close ancestral spirits of hallows' night,
*   Gather around my cauldron light.*
For all across the land, Death does roam,
*   But here the Lord protects his own.*

Place the apples around the cauldron. Light the candle inside the cauldron and do the Invocation of the God and then the Invocation of the Goddess. After the invocations, take time to do some divination or meditation on the meaning of the ritual. Next, energize the protection bag you made. Place your hands over the bag, express your desire, and then chant the following:

Blithe spirits' blessing, from cauldron light,
Protect me now, with all your might.

Pause, then bless the wine or cider through the Rite of Union and the bread through the Blessing of the Bread ceremony. Begin your closing segment of the rite by offering this blessing:

Within my heart is devoted feeling
   Vainly should my lips express.
I come before your altar kneeling
   And pray this time and place you bless.

Beginning in the North, extinguish the candles in the pumpkins as follows:

North

Death now brings darkness to the North, the home of the final atonement.

West

Death now brings darkness to the West, the home of rest and regeneration.

South

Death now brings darkness to the South, the home of the divine spark.

East

Death now brings darkness to the East, the home of the eternal spirit.

Dismiss the Guardians and extinguish the altar candles, beginning with the left:

Left

Blessed be Death Crone
Transform my soul this night.

Right

Blessed be Lord of Death
Bring me rest and quiet.

Take up the circle and allow the floating candle and the black pillar candle to burn out. Place the protection bag where you feel it will do the most good, such as in your car, in your desk at work, or in a special place at home.

Yule: The Winter Solstice

Yule is a pre-Christian holiday celebrated on the winter solstice, which falls around December 21. It is the true new year, both astronomically and spiritually. At this time, we see the simultaneous death and rebirth of the Sun God, represented in the shortest day and longest night of the year. From this time forward, the sun grows in power and strength.

To our ancestors, from where our teachings come, fertility was an important aspect of daily life. As the sun is vital for growth and fertility, it is only natural that its return was celebrated with elaborate rituals and ceremonies.

Though we don't necessarily use the Sabbat rites for fertility in a physical sense, the energy is still there and can be tapped into.

Yule is the time to begin to think about what you want to accomplish in the months to come. It is the time to outline the goals you wish to work towards. As the Sabbats progress, you will refine and narrow down these goals in content and purpose. For now you want to focus your attention inward to allow your higher self or spiritual side time to clarify what needs to be done and which goals to set. Ask for guidance from the God and Goddess.

Ritual Tools, Symbols, and Decorations

Altar decorations: Red altar cloth, red or green altar candles, sprigs of holly tied with red and green ribbons, bayberry candle, poinsettia plant, wand tied with red and green ribbon, chalice covered with a gold cloth, red and white wine, ritual cakes.

Plants and herbs: Bayberry, bay laurel, oak, mistletoe, orange, cinnamon, frankincense, poinsettia, pine tree, juniper, myrrh, anise, and red and white carnations.

Oil: Mix orange, cinnamon, and bayberry oils together for anointing, or use frankincense and myrrh.

Food: Gingerbread, plum pudding, sugar cookies, fruit cake, roast goose or duck, turkey, roast beef, mincemeat, root vegetables.

Symbols: Yule log, mistletoe tied with green ribbon, Yule tree decorated with colorful ornaments and lights, gifts wrapped in bright seasonal paper, bowl filled with fresh fruits and nuts, wand tied with red and green ribbon, talismans to represents personal desires and goals.

A Ceremony for Yule

Light the right altar candle and then the left one as you say the following:

Right

Blessed be the fire of faith, which brings forth the light.

Left

Blessed be the light of the world, which brings forth life.

Cast the circle and call in the Guardians. Face the altar, anoint the forehead with seasonal oil, and speak the following blessing:

Blessed be the White Goddess,
Blessed be the sacrificed King
Blessed be the spiritual seed
Blessed be the new born Sun.

Say the following blessing and light the bayberry candle:

Lord and lady of the night,
    Of mist and of moonlight,
Though you are seldom seen
    I meet you in heart, mind, and dream.
Bless my thoughts, works, and deeds,
    That they shall fulfill my wishes and needs.
On this night I honor thee
    To make my desire a reality,
My love I now give to thee
    For your blessings, So Mote It Be!

Offer the candle at each of the four quadrants as you speak accordingly:

East

Blessed be the light coming from the East that brings insight and wisdom.

South

Blessed be the fire coming from the South that brings strength and power.

West

Blessed be the moisture coming from the West that brings control and dominion.

North

Blessed the fertile earth of the North that provides manifestation of desire.

Place the candle back on the altar. Take a few moments to meditate on the meaning of the ritual. Relax. Invoke the God, and then invoke the Goddess. At this point you will want to energize the bayberry candle with your thoughts and desires. Place your hands over the candle, express your desire, and then chant the following:

God of glory, God of light
Bless me on this solstice night.

Pause and then bless the wine and bread through the Rite of Union and the Blessing of the Bread ceremony. Begin your closing segment of the rite by offering this blessing:

Within my heart is devoted feeling
Vainly should my lips express,
I come before your altar kneeling
And pray this time and place you bless.

Dismiss the Guardians and extinguish the altar candles, beginning with the left:

Left

Blessed be the faith that brought forth light.

Right

Blessed be the light that brought forth life.

Take up the circle and allow the bayberry candle to burn out.

Imbolg (Brigantia)

 Imbolg, or Brigantia, is celebrated on February 1. This is the feast of the waxing light or the feast of lights, and is related to the Goddess Bridget or Bride. Imbolg is associated with the return of life and light and marks the awakening of the earth and the promise of spring.

In Greece, during the Eleusinian Mysteries, people held a torchlight procession on February 1 in honor of Demeter. The torchlight was to aid her in her search for her lost daughter, Persephone. When Persephone was found, light returned to the world. In Pagan religious tradition this is the time when the virgin-maiden aspect of the Goddess is courted by the young Lord God. Their passion for each other is felt in the seasonal energy at this time. Closely related to Imbolg is the Christian festival of Candlemas, which is celebrated on February 2 and is a time of purification.

Imbolg is the time to prepare for what you wish to accomplish in the months to come. At this time, you will want to clarify and refine what you began to work on at Yule. Use a rose-colored candle to help energize and reaffirm your goal.

Ritual Tools, Symbols, and Decorations

Altar decorations: White, silver, or pink altar cloth, white altar candles, bouquet of pink rosebuds tied with silver ribbon, rose-colored candle, wand tied with pink and silver ribbon, chalice covered with a silver or white cloth, white wine, ritual cakes.

Plants and herbs: Rose, baby's breath, vanilla, jasmine, angelica, heather, basil, blackberry, iris, myrrh, and violet.

Oil: Mix rose, jasmine, and violet oil together for anointing; add a sprig of heather to the master bottle.

Food: Custard, lamb, butter, yogurt, cheese, fish, biscuits, candid violets, Irish stew, leek soup, lentils.

Symbols: Bridget's cross, crown of candles, candles engraved with pink or silver hearts, heart shaped boxes decorated with pink roses to place wishes in, white lace potpourri pouches filled with violet, rose, and heather and tied with pink ribbon, clear quartz crystals.

A Ceremony for Imbolg

Light the right altar candle and then the left one, as you say the following:

Right

Fearless Lord, protector, and father of all,
Bring forth light, life, and wisdom.

Left

White maiden, gentle mother, silent one,
Deliver us from ignorance and darkness.

Cast the circle and call in the Guardians. Face the altar, anoint the forehead with seasonal oil, and speak the following blessing:

My lady who has been with me from the beginning
You are my light and life.
My Lord who comes from the glory of the lady
You are my strength and power.
Let now the dawn and spring of life come forth.
Let now the fire and spirit of life come forth.
Let now the passion and love of life come forth.
Let now the balance and wisdom of life come forth.

Light the rose-colored candle as you say the following:

I pray, banish the winter and bring back the spring,
Let the light and life come to every living thing.
The glory of the God and Goddess I now behold,
For all that is given shall return threefold.
As I revel in the warmth of this divine light,
I pray, bless and protect me from this night.

Pick up the bouquet of flowers and hold them in offering as you say:

Lady of light, wise one thou art pure in spirit
And love eternal.
Lord of fire, passionate one thou art true force
And endless power.

Place the bouquet on the altar in front of the candle. Take a few moments to meditate on the meaning of the ritual.

Relax. Invoke the God and then Invoke the Goddess. At this point you will want to energize the rose-colored candle with your thoughts and desires. Place your hands over the candle, express your desire, and then chant the following:

> *Passion and fire*
> *Bring forth desire.*

Pause and then bless the wine and bread through the Rite of Union and the Blessing of the Bread ceremony. Begin your closing segment of the rite by offering this blessing:

> *Within my heart is devoted feeling*
> *Vainly should my lips express.*
> *I come before your altar kneeling*
> *And pray this time and place you bless.*

Dismiss the Guardians and extinguish the altar candles, beginning with the left:

Left

> *Lady of light, wise one, thou art pure spirit*
> *And love eternal.*

Right

> *Lord of fire, passionate one, thou art true force*
> *And endless power.*

Take up the circle and allow the rose-colored candle to burn out. Dry the pink rose buds in the bouquet and use in incense.

Ostara: The Spring Equinox

 The spring equinox is celebrated around March 21. This is the time when the sun crosses the plane of the equator, making day and night of equal length. This is the actual beginning of spring and the agricultural season. In fact, most of our modern day Easter customs come from the older, Pagan, Ostara festival. The most popular of these practices is decorating eggs. In ancient Egypt, Rome, Greece, and Persia, brightly colored eggs, symbolic of immortality, fertility, and resurrection, were eaten at this time.

The spring equinox is a time of balance, equality, and harmony, between the masculine and feminine forces in nature. This is also the time when you physically, as well as symbolically, plant the seeds of your desires. The plants that grow from the seeds will represent what you are working for. When the plant bears fruit at harvest, so, too, should your desire manifest in physical form.

The first physical step in the process is to plant a seed that symbolizes your desire. For example, use marigolds for prosperity, basil for love, thyme for health, and bittersweet for protection. Place your seeds in a plastic Easter egg, bless them during ritual, and then plant them.

A Ceremony for Ostara

Light the right altar candle and then the left one, as you say the following:

Right

> *Lord of the sky now descend,*
> *Move the spirit of my soul.*
> *Renew within the vital force,*
> *Give me energy, make me whole.*

Ritual Tools, Symbols, and Decorations

Altar decorations: Lilac or pastel blue altar cloth, lilac or pastel blue altar candles, lilies tied with lilac ribbon, lilac-scented pillar candle, wand tied with lilac or pale blue ribbon, chalice covered with a lilac or pale blue cloth, rose wine, egg shaped container filled with seeds for blessing.

Plants and herbs: Iris, dogwood, cinquefoil, lily, daffodil, dittany of Crete, mint, orris, violet, daisy, primrose, sweet pea.

Oil: Mix lily, violet, and sweet pea together for anointing, add a sprig of mint or a violet to the master bottle.

Food: Eggs, custard, biscuits, lamb, chicken, ham, mint tea, peas, fruit compote, poppyseed cake, mustard greens, squash, leafy green salad with sprouts.

Symbols: Decorated eggs, baskets filled with eggs, egg shaped boxes, rabbits, bouquets of lilies tied with lilac and white ribbon, wildflower chain necklaces, seeds, and packages of seeds tied together with yellow and light green ribbon.

Left

> *Lady from the earth now come,*
>   *Lead me into the new dawning day.*
> *Protect me from the passions of man,*
>   *Guide me along thy secret way.*

Cast the circle and call in the Guardians. Face the altar, anoint the forehead with seasonal oil, and light the lilac-scented pillar candle as you speak the following blessing:

By the power of Air, Fire, Water, and Earth
To spring and joy O Goddess give birth.

Pick up the lilac-scented candle and offer it at each of the quadrants. Begin in the East by saying:

East

Element of Air, power of the mind,
Your intellect and wisdom I now bind.

South

Element of Fire, power of the soul,
Your strength and fortitude make me whole.

West

Element of Water, power of the heart,
Your beauty and grace now impart.

North

Element of Earth, power of the will,
Your force and focus within me still.

Place the candle in the center of the altar. Pick up the egg and ask the following blessing:

White maiden, enchantress, Goddess of Fire
Mother of hearth, home, and desire.
You form the passion within the great God's heart,
So that within you the seed of life he does impart.
O great lady, you are the queen of spring
As you bring light and life to every living thing.

Place the egg filled with the seeds on the altar in front of the candle. Take a few moments to meditate on the meaning of the ritual. Relax. Invoke the Goddess and then invoke the God. At this point you will want to energize the lilac candle with your thoughts and desires. Place your hands over the candle, express your desire, and then chant the following:

> *Blessed be the flower and seed*
> *That will grant to me what I need.*

Pause and bless the wine and bread through the Rite of Union and the Blessing of the Bread ceremony. Begin your closing segment of the rite by offering this blessing:

> *Within my heart is devoted feeling*
> *Vainly should my lips express.*
> *I come before your altar kneeling*
> *And pray this time and place you bless.*

Pick up the candle and proceed to offer it at each of the quadrants in closing. Begin in the North by saying:

North

> *May the spirit of Earth bring me wisdom.*

West

> *May the spirit of Water bring me control.*

South

> *May the spirit of Fire bring me inspiration.*

East

> *May the spirit of Air bring me awareness.*

Dismiss the Guardians and extinguish the altar candles beginning with the left one:

Left

> *Lady, enchantress, mother of the Earth*
> *To my dreams and wishes give birth.*

Right

> *Lord, father of light, glowing sun,*
> *Let my will and work be done.*

Take up the circle, and allow the lilac-scented candle to burn out. When the weather permits, take the seeds out of the plastic egg and plant them. Save the egg to use again next year.

Beltane: May Eve

Beltane is celebrated on April 30 (May Eve), and is primarily a fire and fertility festival. The name, which means "Bel fire," is derived from the Celtic god Bel, also known as Beli or Balor, whose name simply means "Lord." Beltane is also the time of the May queen, when a young woman was chosen from the village to represent the Earth Goddess and reflect the transformation of maiden to mother. This was also the time of the kindling of the need fire, when all fires in the village were extinguished and then ritually re-lit the following day.

Fertility played an important role in the Beltane celebrations. The principle symbol of this Sabbat was the Maypole, also known as the axis mundi, around which the universe revolved. The pole personified the thrusting masculine force, and the disk at the top depicted the receptive female. There were seven colored ribbons tied to it, which represented the seven colors of the rainbow. Fire and fertility, primarily dominated the rituals at this time.

Beltane is when we actively begin to pursue our goals on the material plane. Now is the time to take action and physically put effort into the goal you began to think about at Yule. Make a crown of flowers to represent your aspirations and to bring down the power of the Goddess to aid you in your work.

Ritual Tools, Symbols, and Decorations

Altar decorations: Green altar cloth, green altar candles, vases filled with fresh flowers, small crown of fresh flowers, green pillar candle, wand tied with seven different colored ribbons, chalice covered with green cloth, May wine, and ritual cakes. (To make May wine, add one cup fresh, crushed woodruff leaves to a bottle of semi-sweet white wine, and allow to sit for 30 days. Before serving, garnish with fresh orange and lemon slices.)

Plants and herbs: Almond, belladonna, bluebells, clover, frankincense, marigold, meadowsweet, lily of the valley, rose, rowan, woodruff.

Oil: Mix lily of the valley and rose together for anointing, add a clover or bluebell to the master bottle.

Food: Woodruff wine, fresh strawberries, roasted pork, almond cake, salmon, green beans with almonds, mixed green salad, glazed game hens, oatmeal cakes, quiche.

Symbols: Maypole, the wand, crown of flowers, candles tied with seven different colored ribbons, baskets of fresh flowers tied with colored ribbon, branches of rowan tied with green ribbon, green candle in a cauldron, bonfires.

A Ceremony for Beltane

Light the right altar candle and then the left one, as you say the following:

Right

> Blessed be the Lord of light and power,
> He transforms my soul from this hour.

Left

> Blessed be the lady of love and passion,
> My heart and future she shall fashion.

Cast the circle and call in the Guardians. Face the altar, anoint the forehead with seasonal oil, and speak the following blessing:

> I pray, glorious Goddess of the Moon,
>   As I stand between day and night.
> Your heavenly presences grant me a soon,
>   As darkness gives way to light.

Light the green pillar candle. Pick up the candle and hold it as an offering as you speak the following:

> Thou who rises from the raging sea,
>   Shall now accept thy destiny.
> Now, great lady of the inner Earth,
>   To the land of promise come and give birth.
> So that all the seed, fruit, and grain,
>   Shall in abundance come forth again.

Pick up the crown of flowers, hold it in offering as you invoke the Goddess, then place the crown of flowers on your head. Pick up the wand and invoke the God. Still holding the wand, proceed to each quadrant and ask for blessing. Begin in the East by saying:

East

> *I ask for guidance from the realm of the eternal spirit*
> *Bless me with inspiration and insight.*

South

> *I ask for guidance from the realm of the divine spark*
> *Bless me with energy and power.*

West

> *I ask for guidance form the realm of the final atonement*
> *Bless me with wisdom and control.*

North

> *I ask for guidance from the realm of the ultimate creation*
> *Bless me with skill and ability.*

Place the crown of flowers on the altar. Set the green pillar candle inside the crown and place the wand in front of them. Place your hands over the candle and express your desire, and then chant the following:

> *Lovely lady of the moon*
> *Grant my needs and wishes soon.*

Pause and bless the wine and bread through the Rite of Union and the Blessing of the Bread ceremony. Begin your closing segment of the rite by offering this blessing:

> *Within my heart is devoted feeling*
> *Vainly should my lips express.*
> *I come before your altar kneeling*
> *And pray this time and place you bless.*

Dismiss the Guardians and extinguish the altar candles, beginning with the left:

Left

Blessed shall be this time of enlightenment
My seeds have been sown and my labors shall be
rewarded.

Right

Blessed shall be the rewards of the spirit
May I always remember to give as I have received.

Take up the circle and allow the green pillar candle to
burn out. When the candle has burned out, take the crown
of flowers to a river or stream. Toss the crown into the water, asking the Goddess to bless your goals and help you
manifest your desire.

Midsummer: Summer Solstice

The summer solstice is celebrated
around June 21 and is the longest day
and shortest night of the year. The
festival of the summer solstice is concerned with both fire and water, as
from this point onward, the sun will
decline in its power. The symbol of fire
represents keeping the sun alive. The wa-
ter element is used for the ritual blessing of individuals, sacred wells, and springs.

One of the customs of our ancestors was the leaping
over or passing through fires. It was believed that the higher
they jumped, the higher the crops would grow. As in Beltane,
during the summer solstice cattle were driven through fires
for purification and fumigation. It was also believed that
the fire repelled the powers of evil and would protect the
cattle and all who passed through it.

Another symbol used at this time was the wheel. The turning of the wheel suggests the turning, or progression, of the seasons. Our ancestors decorated wheels with flowers and then placed lighted candles on them. These were then taken to a body of water and set afloat. Symbolically, midsummer is the time to nurture your goals or efforts. That which you have been working for should now be within range. Use a floating candle to give you ambition (fire), and emotional control (water) for your goal.

Ritual Tools, Symbols, and Decorations

Altar decorations: Bright yellow altar cloth, sunshine yellow altar candles, bouquet of marigolds tied with yellow and green ribbon, wand tied with yellow ribbon, floating candle in a bowl of water, chalice covered with a yellow cloth, red and white wine, sun shaped ritual cakes.

Plants and herbs: Chamomile, chickweed, cinquefoil, dogwood, fennel, lavender, mugwort, St. John's wort, vervain, orange, lemon, verbena, sunflower, marigold, dandelion.

Oil: Mix lemon verbena, orange, and lavender oil together for anointing; place marigold petals in the master bottle.

Food: Oranges, lemons, sunflower seeds, avocado, grilled pork and chicken, baked beans, three bean salad, fruit salad, berry pie, potato salad, cucumber and tomato relish, lemon squares.

Symbols: Wheel tied with colored ribbon, floating candles in bowls of colored water, wands made of oak or hawthorn, birds, horned animals, the chariot; sun talismans made of gold, bonfires, wishing wells, and fountains.

A Ceremony for Midsummer

Light the right altar candle and then the left one, as you say the following:

Right

> *Lord of the Sun, God of truth and might*
> *In your honor, do I this candle light.*

Left

> *Lady of the Moon, Goddess of celestial power*
> *I beseech thee to bless me from this hour.*

Cast the circle and call in the Guardians. Face the altar and light the floating candle, pick up the bowl with the candle in it, and proceed to the Eastern Quadrant. Address the Eastern Quadrant as you hold the bowl in offering, and then proceed to the next quadrant. Each time hold the bowl in offering as you say the appropriate line:

East

> *Let now the winds of consciousness bring forth insight*
> *and wisdom.*

South

> *Let now the fires of awareness bring forth motivation*
> *and inspiration.*

West

> *Let now the waves of completeness bring forth love and*
> *understanding.*

North

> *Let now the blossoming, fertile earth bring forth the manifestation of desire.*

Place the bowl back on the altar. Turn, face the Southern Quadrant, and say:

> *To the great Lord of the Sun*
> > *My gratitude I do show.*
> *As in life and spirit*
> > *I work to progress and grow.*
> *I thank you, father of light*
> > *By each and every work and deed.*
> *That all I have and shall receive*
> > *Is all that I shall ever want or need.*

Now, turn and face the altar and do the Invocation of the God and the Invocation of the Goddess. Take a moment to meditate on the meaning of the ritual and season. At this point you will want to energize the floating candle with your own wishes. Place your hands over the candle, express your desire, and then chant the following.

> *Sun and flame*
> *Bring joy and gain.*

Pause, then bless the wine and bread through the Rite of Union and the Blessing of the Bread ceremony. Begin the closing segment of the rite by offering this blessing:

> *Within my heart is devoted feeling*
> > *Vainly should my lips express.*
> *I come before your altar kneeling*
> > *And pray this time and place you bless.*

Dismiss the Guardians, and extinguish the altar candles, beginning with the left:

Left

> *Lady of the Moon, goddess of celestial power*
> *I bid thee bless and protect me from this hour.*

Right

> *Lord of the Sun, god of truth and might*
> *Guide and guard me as I go into the night.*

Take up the circle and allow the floating candle to burn out.

Lughnasadh: Lammas

The festival of Lughnasadh (Celtic), or Lammas (Christian), is held on August 1. The word Lughnasadh is associated with the god Lugh, and the festival was held to commemorate his marriage. Lammas is derived from the Old English *hlafmoesse,* meaning "loaf-mass," and was held in celebration of the first loaves baked from the first grain harvested. The loaves were taken to the local church, where they were blessed by priests. The loaves were then distributed among the congregation. Observing this festival ensured an abundance of fruit and grain for the months to come. The first fruit picked or sheaf cut was considered to be sacred to the Old Gods, and was therefore treated in a special manner.

Corn and grain are the predominant features of rituals at this time because they symbolize the fertility of the earth, the awakening of life, and life coming from death. The golden ears of corn are seen as the offspring of the marriage of the sun and virgin earth. Corn and wine, like bread and wine, represent humankind's labor and ability to sustain life.

Wine- and candle- making were also important features of this time of year, along with preserving food and making other preparations for winter. Other customs include decorating water wells with vines and the blessing of food.

Lughnasadh is the first harvest, when the first sign of the rewards of your labors should be evident. Now is the time to continue working toward your goal, knowing it will be realized. Bring fresh corn to your circle for blessing. This will help reinforce your desire to achieve your goal.

Ritual Tools, Symbols, and Decorations

Altar decorations: Gold or yellow altar cloth, gold altar candles, four ears of corn, each tied with a yellow and orange ribbon, small basket of fruit, gold colored pillar candle, chalice covered with a yellow cloth, red and white wine, corn bread, or ritual cakes.

Plants and herbs: Corn, barley, wheat, rye, fenugreek, frankincense, oats, sunflower, oak, hollyhock, heather, lilac.

Oil: Mix lilac oil with a small amount of corn oil for anointing.

Food: Corn bread, corn on the cob, freshly baked wheat or rye bread, grilled chicken and beef, roast pork, fruit salad, mixed green salad with sprouts and sunflower seeds, baked beans, bread pudding, fresh green beans, peas, and wild rice.

Symbols: Corn; the pentacle; bread and all baked goods; the hearth, broom, and things connected with the home; baskets filled with corn and fresh vegetables; baskets of baked goods tied with gold ribbons; dried corn husks for making corn dolls.

A Ceremony for Lughnasadh

Light the right altar candle and then the left one, as you say the following:

Right

> My Lord is the passion
> He brings forth the light
> The harvest is of his seed.

Left

> My Lady is the power
> She brings forth the life
> The harvest is her reward.

Cast the circle and call in the Guardians. Face the altar and speak the following blessing:

> My lady, I know that naught receives naught,
> That I shall reap that which I have sowed.
> On this night, shall I receive accordingly,
> Fort nothing is withheld from those deserving.
> Blessed shall be the Goddess,
> And blessed shall be the fruits of my labor.

Pick up the four ears of corn. Hold them in offering and ask the following blessing on them:

> Corn and grain are of this earth,
>   With love and work I gave them birth.
> Though they were once just small seeds,
>   Through them I achieved my wishes and needs.

Hold the corn in offering and then place one ear of corn at each of the four quadrants, chanting:

> As the corn, I am reborn.

Offer the corn to the East, and place it next to the eastern quadrant candle. Then proceed to the South, continuing to chant the above ("As the corn, I am reborn"). Do the same for the West and the North. Then return to the altar.

Say the following blessing and light the gold pillar candle:

My Lord and Lady you shall provide
  Long after all has withered and died.
Though you have given me life through the land

What I now hold is the work of my hand.
  I shall always remember, just as the corn,
That I am ever living, dying, and reborn.

As the corn, I am reborn!

Place the candle in the center of the altar on the pentacle, and do the Invocation of the God and the Invocation of the Goddess. Take a moment to meditate on the meaning of the ritual and season. At this point you will want to energize the candle with your own wishes. Place your hands over the candle, express your desire, and then chant the following.

Corn and grain
Bring joy and gain!

Pause, then bless the wine and bread through the Rite of Union and the Blessing of the Bread ceremony. Begin the closing segment of the rite by offering this blessing:

Within my heart is devoted feeling
  Vainly should my lips express.
I come before your altar kneeling
  And pray this time and place you bless.

Dismiss the Guardians and extinguish the altar candles, beginning with the left:

Left

Blessed be the maiden, mother, and crone
Bring me blessings from your harvest home.

Right

Blessed be the king of corn and grain
As now the season of abundance begins to wane.

Take up the circle and allow the gold candle to burn out. Hang the ears of corn to dry. When the ears of corn have completely dried, save them to make your Corn-baba, a doll made from dried corn husks used during the autumnal equinox celebration.

Mabon: Autumnal Equinox

 The autumnal equinox, also known as Mabon, is celebrated sometime around September 21. Again, as with the spring equinox, we have a time of equal day and equal night. However, after this night, the days grow shorter and the sun begins to wane in power.

This Sabbat is also known as The Harvest Home and is basically the end of the agricultural year. Now all the crops have been gathered. Canning and storage for the winter is a priority, and wine-making is in full progress. Some things that come to mind are leaves turning color, bird migrations, corn harvesting, and bonfires.

The purpose of celebrating the autumnal equinox is twofold. First, we want to give thanks for all our blessings and achievements, and second, we want to project for the ability to maintain that which we possess. It does no good to manifest a goal if you cannot hold on to it. This is what the Corn-baba represents — thanksgiving for what you have received, and request for the ability to keep what you have created. (For an easy Corn-baba, you can tie multicolored ribbons around an ear of corn to represent the corn mother, or place an ear of corn in a basket decorated with dried flowers and brightly colored ribbons.)

Ritual Tools, Symbols, and Decorations

Altar decorations: Orange, red, or brown altar cloth; orange or red altar candles; Corn-baba; cornucopia filled with fruit and vegetables; a red, apple-shaped candle; a wand tied with orange, red, and brown ribbons, apple-flavored wine or hard cider; ritual cakes.

Plants and herbs: Apples, acorn, benzoin, honeysuckle, cinnamon, clove, nutmeg, marigold, myrrh, blessed thistle, gourds, fern.

Oil: Mix cinnamon, clove, and myrrh oils together for anointing.

Food: Corn, apples, apple pie, baked pork with apples, cinnamon cookies, glazed game hens, ginger bread, Indian pudding, baked potatoes, sweet potatoes, Waldorf salad, mixed vegetables, cider, mulled wine, corn fritters, green bean casserole.

Symbols: Corn baba, apples, scarecrow, cornucopia, sickle, dried gourds, broom, cauldron, apple dolls, dried flowers, leaves, bonfires, and baskets tied with orange, red, and brown ribbons.

At this point, your goal should have manifested or at least be well within your reach. Technically, this is a time to give thanks for all the blessings you have received throughout the year.

A Ceremony for Mabon

Light the right altar candle and then the left one, as you say the following:

Right

> *Lord of the Sun*
> > *Pulsing bright,*
> *Cast away the shadows*
> > *Bring forth the light.*

Left

> *Lady of the Moon*
> > *Jewel of power*
> *Bless this sacred space*
> > *From this hour.*

Cast the circle, and call in the Guardians. Face the altar, anoint the forehead with seasonal oil, and speak the following blessing:

> *Blessed be the Lady.*
> *Blessed be the Lord.*
> *Blessed be the corn.*
> *Blessed be the harvest.*

Say the following blessing, and light the apple candle:

Lord of corn, barley, and rye,
  Golden sun, ruler of the sky.
Lady of milk, honey, and wine
  Silver moon, mistress most divine.
Fruit of field, passion, and fire,
  Light the way, fulfill desire.
Blessed be the Lord and Lady!

Place the candle back on the altar and pick up the Corn-baba. Hold the Corn-baba in offering as you ask this blessing:

Golden-haired mother
  Red dying king
Leaves are falling
  And sickles gleam.
Hearty is the harvest
  Blessed is the corn
What withers and dies
  Always is reborn.

Still holding the Corn-baba, proceed to offer it at each of the quadrants. Begin in the East by saying:

East

Element of Air, power of the mind,
Your intellect and wisdom I now bind.

South

Element of Fire, power of the soul,
Your strength and fortitude make me whole.

West

Element of Water, power of the heart,
Your beauty and grace now impart.

North

Element of Earth, power of the will,
Your force and focus within me still.

Place the Corn-baba in the center of the altar and do the Invocation of the God and then the Invocation of the Goddess. Take a moment to meditate on the meaning of the ritual and season. At this point you will want to energize the Corn-baba with your own wishes. Place your hands over the Corn-baba, express your desire, and then chant the following:

Blessed be the harvest
    Blessed be the home
Blessed be the grain
    And all that I have sown.

Pause, and bless the wine or cider through the Rite of Union, and the bread with the Blessing of the Bread ceremony. Begin your closing segment of the rite by offering this blessing:

Within my heart is devoted feeling
    Vainly should my lips express.
I come before your altar kneeling
    And pray this time and place you bless.

Pick up the Corn-baba and proceed to offer it in closing at each of the quadrants. Begin in the North by saying:

North

May the spirit of earth bring me wisdom.

West

May the spirit of water bring me control.

South

May the spirit of fire bring me inspiration.

East

May the spirit of air bring me awareness.

Dismiss the Guardians and extinguish the altar candles, beginning with the left one:

Left

> *Lady of the silver moon,*
> > *Mistress of this holy earth.*
> *Grant to me a special boon,*
> > *To my wishes and needs give birth.*

Right

> *Lord of the golden sun,*
> > *Master of the forest and field.*
> *Let your will and work be done,*
> > *Protect me with your sword and shield.*

Take up the circle and allow the apple candle to burn out. Hang the Corn-baba over the main entrance to your home. If you own a business and want to increase sales, place the Corn-baba next to the cash register.

This completes the eight Wiccan Sabbats. It is through these rites and other celebrations based on nature that the Witch is able to express his or her magickal desires and appreciation for the God and Goddess. The ceremonies presented here are not written in stone, nor are they the only way to approach seasonal celebration. They are simply guidelines to inspire creativity when approaching the seasonal shifts. If you plan to expand these rituals for group work, be sure your additions go well with the basic framework and seasonal focus of the rite. Always keep in mind the influence of the energies that will be available at the time of your ceremony. Work with, not against, the ebb and flow of the natural forces of the universe. When you align your power and energy with that of Mother Nature, you will prosper and grow.

Chapter 11

Wicca and Magick

"Magick is the art of making changes in reality by acts of Will and Imagination. Magick could be said to be the Art, encompassing all other arts; it is a way of creating the world."
—Bill Whitcomb, *The Magician's Companion*

Witchcraft is the celebration of life, and magick is the ability to control it. Magick is the one thing that can really help improve life, is something everyone can do, and is only as good or evil as the person using it. Magick is a science that brings those who practice it into alignment with the natural forces of the universe. By using the powers of the mind, in combination with certain objects, the magician manipulates the forces of the universe to bend or change reality according to his or her own will.

Magick, like any philosophy, has infinite possibilities, as well as distinct limitations. It relies heavily on the strength of character and mental ability of the individual using it. Magick also depends on belief much more than it does on intent. What you really, truly believe is what will come into being—not what you simply want. If you don't believe in what you are doing, then all the spells, candles, and incantations in the world will not work.

The Principles of Magick

As a science, magick has certain principles that are at the heart of its mechanics. The first principle is the Principle of Similarity. The second is the Principle of Contact or Contagion. Both of these principles come under the designation of Sympathetic Magick.

The Principle of Similarity is also referred to as Homeopathic or Imitative Magick. It states that like produces like, or that an effect may resemble its cause. Simply put, whatever you do to the symbolic representation of a person, place, or thing will directly affect that same person, place, or thing.

A good example of homeopathic magick is the Voodoo doll, created by practitioners when they wish to influence someone. The doll is fashioned to look like the person they wish to influence. Then, depending upon the circumstances, the practitioners will proceed to heal or hurt their targeted victims through magickal conjurations. Because the dolls look like (imitate) the intended victims, they are capable of creating a link with them. The intentions of the practitioner then travel through the link, impacting what is at the other end.

In partnership with the principle of Similarity is the principle of Contact or Contagion. This principle states that things that have been in contact with each other will continue to act on each other, even at a distance, after all physical contact has been broken. Because of this, it is possible to use a person's picture, clothing, or handwriting as a magickal link. These links are often referred to as "lag-locks" or "relics," and are of primary importance in certain spells and enchantments, especially when love and friendship are involved. As in homeopathic magick, what is done to the link will create an effect on the intended target.

The Four Cornerstones of Magick

In addition to the principles of Similarity and Contagion, most practitioners adhere to the four cornerstones of magick. These four principles are expressed in the ability *to know, to will, to dare,* and *to keep silent.*

1. To Know

This refers to knowledge about magick and what makes it work. The practitioner must know and understand the basic working principles of a magickal operation before he or she attempts it. There is a saying in magick that knowledge is power, so if the practitioner wants power, then he or she must first have knowledge.

2. To Will

This is the ability to concentrate, focus attention, and direct the will to manifest desire. Practitioners must be able to force their will upon the universe, in a positive and powerful way, to accomplish their desires. In magick, practitioners must be able to control their surroundings, which include the mind and body.

3. To Dare

This is the courage to challenge ideas. Magicians must be able to stand up for what they believe in and be able to demand their rights. They must dare to have the courage to make their will manifest desire, without fear or doubt. The magician must be able to command respect from his or her peers, as well as from the forces with which they work. They must dare to be strong.

4. To Keep Silent

This is by far the hardest of the four rules. The practitioner must shut out, and off, all outside distractions and learn to concentrate and focus. Silence also has a partner, the mouth. The well-trained magician knows how to keep it shut and not crow about every little thing she does. This is because every time she speaks of the magickal works she is doing, she dissipates her energy and power. This is why you don't hear Witches and magicians bragging about what they did or are doing.

The Magickal Process

Creative Visualization

One of the most important aspects of any magickal work is creative visualization. It is considered to be the key to success and personal power. Creative visualization is a process or technique used for making dreams and wishes come true. In essence, creative visualization is a fancy name for the old children's game of "let's pretend."

The magician creates an image in his or her mind of a person, place, or thing that he or she desires to have or to affect. This image is then empowered through magickal incantations and then acted upon during ritual. The psychic energy directed toward the mind image causes it to physically manifest.

There are three guidelines, comparable to the Witch's Pyramid, that the magician follows when using creative visualization. These guidelines, belief, desire, and visualization, are referred to as the *Witch's Mystical Triangle.*

The Witch's Mystical Triangle

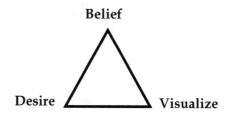

Guideline One: Belief

This is a very important guideline. Practitioners must believe in their goals or objects of desire if they are going to achieve them. There is a saying that what you believe can happen, you can make happen. Witches and magicians know they must have faith. They must believe in their personal power if they are going to get anywhere in magick or life.

Guideline Two: Desire

There must be a strong desire. You won't see competent Witches or magicians sitting around wishing for this or that. If there is something they need or desire, they use their powers to get it. They will be obsessed with their goal. This obsession stirs their emotions into action and gives them the power to achieve.

Guideline Three: Visualize

This is the most important guideline of all. Practitioners must be able to create a clear mental picture or duplicate image of their desires in their minds. They must be able to see the thing they desire, just as if they were looking at a photograph. Being able to actually see, within the mind, what they want is the key to making it manifest.

Practicing Witches or magicians will take photographs, draw, and even visit and/or touch the object of their desire. Then, within the bounds of the magick circle, they will recreate mentally what they desire. Through will power and focused energy they visualize their desire into reality.

Astral Projection

The astral plane is the working ground of the magician. It is the level of awareness in the etheric world that is close to the material world. It vibrates faster than the material world but looks similar when viewed clairvoyantly. To the traveler on the astral plane, the scenery and everything connected with it seem as solid as the most solid material appears to the physical eye. The astral plane is just as real to the astral body as the material plane is to the physical body.

In magick, the astral plane is where the truth about all things is revealed. It is the place of angels, demons, and fairies, host to the elemental forces of nature. The astral plane holds the secret of power and the key to the creation of miraculous effects on the physical plane.

Most magicians believe that each thought, idea, or action sets up a vibration on the astral plane. Not only are thoughts and ideas logged onto the astral plane, but so are duplicate images of every object and living thing on earth. The idea is to travel to the astral plane and impress the duplicate image with a desire. The earthly counterpart is then impacted with this desire and reacts accordingly.

The most direct approach to the astral plane is through astral projection. This can be accomplished during the dream state or through conscious out-of-body experience. Before going to bed, the practitioner will program his or her mind to project to a designated place. During this time, the mind will record all it sees and does. Upon awakening, the Witch will immediately record his or her impressions. This procedure will be repeated until the practitioner can leave his or her body consciously while in a state of meditation or relaxation. If the magician can focus his or her attention hard enough, then astral projection will take place. There are several types of imagined suggestion exercises that can be used to aid in the process:

▶ *Visual suggestion:* This involves seeing the self projected astrally onto a higher plane of existence.

▶ *Symbolic suggestion:* This is the ability to visualize an exit point for the astral body, such as a tiny hole or tunnel, and project the consciousness through it.

▶ *Sensation suggestion:* This involves actually feeling the self projecting, or imagining the sensations of projection.

A combination of any or all these techniques can be used for astral projection or the externalizing of consciousness in a controlled manner. One simple exercise that seems to help is setting up a controlled experiment as follows.

Choose a room in your house. Go into the room and look around, studying where everything in the room is. Note the color of the walls, floor, and furniture.

Every day for a week, study the room. Get to know every little thing in it. Then lie down in a quiet place, relax, close your eyes, and imagine yourself walking into the room. Look around. What do you see? Spend about 10 minutes in the room mentally and then leave. Now have someone go into the room and move something or add something. Then lie down again, relax, and mentally enter the room. Look around. What do you see? If you see what has been changed or added, then you're astrally projecting.

Divination

In addition to creative visualization and astral travel, the practitioner of the magickal arts will use divination to help accomplish his or her desire. Divination is the prediction of the future or the discovery of secrets by means of a variety of occult methods. (Because occult means hidden or secret, an occult method is one done in private.) Divination is the process used to pinpoint obstacles so they can be dealt with before they become problems.

The principal force behind divination is Mentality. Mentality is the extension of time, through which the mind is allowed to express itself. The extension of time and expression of the mind can best be explained as inner film stills that can be viewed at any given point by the individual. According to the theory of divination, there is no time or space for the unconscious mind, which is the vehicle of divination. The past, present, and future are all open to the scrutiny of the deep unconscious intelligence that lies within us all.

Witches and magicians believe that all knowledge of the past, present, and future is locked and carefully safeguarded in a secret compartment of the brain. The information stored in this compartment is available to the conscious mind. It is then up to the practitioner to find the key that will open the compartment. The key is contained in the many systems of divination. It is up to the individual to discover which system holds the key that will unlock his or her compartment.

There are many, many ways to divine the future, and it would take a set of encyclopedias to do them all justice, so only the most widely used forms of divination are discussed here.

Cartomancy

Cartomancy is the art of fortune telling with cards. Specifically designed Tarot cards are the choice of most Wiccans. The standard Tarot deck contains 78 cards, including 22 Major Arcana or Trump cards and 56 Lower Arcana or numbered cards.

The pictures on the cards, as well as their numbered position, provoke thoughts and feelings for the reader to explore. A book without words, the Tarot speaks to the reader through a pictorial symbolic language that reveals past and present events.

When used in a proper manner, the Tarot can be startlingly accurate. Of course, as with all forms of divination, accuracy depends on the individual gifts of the diviner and the conditions prevailing at the time.

Crystallomancy

Crystallomancy is the practice of gazing into a crystal ball (or sometimes a bowl of colored water). As the diviner, usually called a seer, gazes into the crystal ball, he or she will allow his or her mind to wander, while physical attention is focused on the ball. The interior of the ball will begin to cloud over, becoming milky in appearance. The milkiness will change color and become darker until it is totally black. Then the blackness will dissolve, like a curtain being pulled aside, and in the center of the ball will be a living picture. The picture will then be interpreted according to individual intuition.

For example, a rabbit or frog in a field of flowers could indicate fertility. If the seer came upon a dark clad figure in a rain-soaked park, it might indicate danger or death. Sometimes only a single object appears such as the sun, which means prosperity, or a moon and star, which can signify travel or imply that the person has mystical abilities.

It would be impossible to attribute a meaning to every symbol or pictorial situation, as so much depends on the intuition and ability of the seer. However, most symbols are interpreted according to their nature. Usually hearts and flowers indicate love or friendship; birds and planes, travel; and food or money, abundance.

Palmistry

Palmistry is another favored form of divination. It is the ability to look at people's hands and read their characters. The shape of the palm, the lines, and the fingers will reveal the individual's past and suggest future events.

It is believed that the outlines of the person's character, fortune, and life are imprinted upon the palm before birth. However, the imprint does not indicate what *must* happen, but rather what will happen if changes in attitude and lifestyle are not made.

The indications in the palm will alter in accordance with the changes the individual makes. When predetermined mistakes are avoided or rectified, those indicating lines will change accordingly. A good reader can see by looking at the hand just what changes have taken place over a period of time and what course of action the individual should take in order to continue to grow and progress.

For example, if a reader sees that a young woman may fall in love at a certain time, the young woman may very well fall in love at this time, but this does not mean she must marry the individual. It is probable that she will do so, but the only certainty is that she will fall in love. She still has the free will to control her own destiny.

The beauty of divination is that it provides information about what will happen if a certain life pattern is followed. All people have the free will to choose to continue with what they are doing and thus fulfill the prophecy. Or they can take heed, avoid the mistakes and pitfalls revealed in the reading, and alter the outcome.

Magick is an art and a science. It gives you the ability to make changes in your life. Through creative visualization and the movement of energy, you are able to manipulate the forces of nature to recreate your reality. Consider magick high-powered, positive thinking that can give you the upper hand in life. Remember: What the mind can imagine, the will can create.

Chapter 12

Spellcrafting and Natural Magick

"The most important ingredient of any spell is love."
—Gillian Kemp, *The Good Spell Book*

A spell is a period of time during which a person or situation is held in a captive state for the benefit of the individual working his or her will and intent. Using special chants, magically charged objects, and specific actions, the quarry is lured into an easily manipulated state of consciousness. Once in a captive state, the person under the spell experiences events and thoughts he or she cannot account for and yet feels are from his or her own personal effort. In most cases spells result in direct and dynamic effects that usually achieve immediate results.

Contrary to popular sentiment, spellcasting is not some sort of demonic activity. It is simply a way to acquire those things most people need and want. Through creative visualization, in combination with certain symbols, the Witch creates a link between him or herself and the object of his or her desire. When the link has been established, it works just like a telephone line, connecting the Witch to his or her desire. Once connected, the Witch is able to manipulate those forces of nature that will ultimately bring his or her desire into manifestation.

Most Witches consider spells to be the simplest and most convenient way to express their magickal will. In essence, spells can be used for just about everything, from creating a passionate love affair to protecting one's property. However, before you cast that lifesaving spell, you should consider the ramifications of your actions. In the long run, will the spell provide what you really need, or is it just a quick fix that might make the problem worse? If there are other people involved, will they benefit as well? Is there some other way to get what you want? These are all questions you should ask before picking up the magick wand and blithely waving it about. Remember the old adage: Be careful what you wish for — you just may get it.

How to Cast a Magick Spell

Proper timing, correct symbolism, and focused attention or creative visualization are the things it takes to make your magick work. The following suggestions will help those just starting out cast truly effective spells.

The first thing you will want to do is to plan your spell to coincide with the proper phases of the moon.

▶   The new moon is used to begin projects, attract money, or regenerate friendships and health.

▶   The full moon is used for work on personal success, career, or love and marriage.

▶   Then the waning moon is used to get rid of negative influences and bad situations.

The next important step is to consider what day of the week will be most advantageous for the spell you are doing (see the chart on page 168). All natural phenomena or energy (especially the seven planets) have the ability to effect a change. When this natural energy is properly channeled, it works with your personal power to create an impact on a desired target. The more natural energy you have to direct toward your goal, the better your chances of crafting a truly potent spell.

After selecting the proper phase of the moon and day of the week, you will want to fashion the spell to imitate the results you hope to achieve. This involves selecting the right symbols and objects to create the appropriate atmospheric conditions that will help activate your spell.

For example, a spell to attract love would enlist symbols that convey love, such as hearts, pink candles, flowers, rings, and a photograph of the loved one. Then a poem or chant would be used to express the intent. The appropriate symbols used in combination with a powerful chant are what create the current of energy that makes the spell work. The energy you put out acts like a laser beamed at a target. The person or object on whom the spell has been cast will be overwhelmed by the current of energy and react accordingly.

Symbols are important because they elicit an automatic reaction and channel creative energy toward a specific goal.

Correspondences for the Days of the Week

Sunday corresponds to the sun. It represents high masculine energy and is a very good time for individual, positive, creative works. Sunday is a good time to begin spells that are aimed at acquiring money, health, friendship, and patronage for business.

Monday aligns with the moon. This is a day of high feminine energy and a good time to develop self-expression, seek inspiration, and work to enhance psychic abilities. Monday is a good time to begin spells that deal with initiating changes and personal growth of the feminine aspect.

Tuesday belongs to Mars, the God of War. This is a time of dynamic energy and pure raw power. Tuesday is a good time to begin spells that will overcome rivalry or malice, develop physical strength and courage, or help protect one's property and investments. It is also a good time for military matters and anything that requires a lot of force, power, and energy to activate.

Wednesday is associated with Mercury and the ability to communicate. Wednesday is a good time to do spells where communication is involved, as Mercury is used to influence others and help them see things your way. Spells that deal with work and career are best done on Wednesday.

Thursday corresponds to the planet Jupiter. It deals with expansion, idealism, and ambition. Jupiter will help you attain friendship. Thursday is a good time to do spells for career success and situations involving money. Legal transactions are best done during Jupiter.

Friday belongs to Venus, the Goddess of Love. All things concerned with love, attraction, friendships, and lust come under the jurisdiction of Venus. Friday is the best time to work spells that involve friendships or sexual attraction.

Saturday is associated with Saturn and the first law of Karma (limitation). In magick, Saturn is the tester, the principle of learning through trial and error. Saturn spells should be used to preserve, stabilize, and crystallize ability — the ability to discipline the self.

They help you draw the energy from within, and then project it outward toward an intended goal. Symbols are the tools Witches use to help to bring their wishes and desires into reality.

Most skilled practitioners of the magickal arts will agree that symbols are the link between desiring and acquiring. Symbols are simple, and most often natural. They allow some people to get what they want, whereas others never seem to succeed. The proper use of symbols goes hand in hand with knowledge, experience, and accomplishment.

In the beginning you should try to incorporate some natural symbolism into your spells. Things like crystals, herbs, incense, and special oils, have natural energy of their own. When these are combined with your natural energy, they have a dynamic effect on your goal. The chart on page 170 will help you choose the right symbols for your spell work.

Talismans

There are a lot of spells and magickal operations that call for the use of a talisman or amulet, so it is a good idea to know something about them.

The word talisman means "to consecrate." It is the process of consecration that converts a mundane object into an effective vehicle for inducing changes to occur in accordance with the will.

According to MacGregor Mathers, a ceremonial magician, author, and founder of the Golden Dawn magickal order, a talisman is "a magickal figure charged with the force it is intended to represent." A talisman is usually constructed to attain a specific result, and its effectiveness is obvious immediately or within seven days of its construction.

Associations and Correspondences for Spellcasting

Association	Color	Plant	Incense	Stone	Tool	Symbol
Creativity	Orange	Verbena	Jasmine	Orange Calcite	Wand	Window
Fertility	Green	Mistletoe	Peach	Pearl	Chalice	Serpent
Friendship	Pink	Sweetpea	Rose	Rose Quartz	Chalice	Door
Gambling	Yellow/Green	Star Anise	Strawberry	Magnet	Pentacle	Hand
Harmony	Pale Blue	Lavender	Lavender	Amethyst	Chalice	Dove
Love	Pink/Red	Rose	Patchouli	Rhodochrosite	Chalice	Heart
Money	Gold/Green	Irish Moss	Pine	Aventurine	Pentacle	Dollar Sign
Passion	Red	Damiana	Vanilla	Carnelian	Chalice	Torch
Power	Red/Purple	Galangal	Galangal	Quartz Crystal	Athame	Fire
Protection	Black/White	Nettle	Frankincense	Onyx	Athame	Fence
Strength	Red/White	Bay	Carnation	Tiger's Eye	Athame	Chain
Success	Gold	Sunflower	Cinnamon	Diamond	Pentacle	Crown

Most Witches and practitioners of the magickal arts make their own talismans. It is believed that magickal objects work best when they have been constructed by the person who will be using them. Since a true talisman is a custom-made artifact, designed for a specific purpose, it is only reasonable that the individual using it should be its creator as well.

The important thing to remember about talismans is that once created and charged, they can be left to do their work — without further attention. This is because the energy set up by the operator continues to work over a set period of time. Talismans work like batteries — once charged, they continue to give off energy. This continual output of energy is due to the relationship between the talisman, its creator, and the corresponding symbolic force it is related to.

Talismans give you the ability to summon forth the cosmic powers of the universe and make it possible for you to extend and intensify your personal magnetism. What makes the talisman such a powerful expression of magickal force is its occult symbolism. Ancient magickal seals, such as those of Solomon, Moses, and David are full not only of original power, but also of the power built into them through thousands of years of use. Talismans reflect the inner universe of human nature, help unlock the powers within us, and provide access to the powers outside of us. As carefully crafted vehicles of magickal force, talismans contain tremendous energy that is of great benefit to their owners.

Personal Power Talisman

Personal power is important because it sustains self-confidence and moral fortitude. It also maintains your self-esteem and helps you bring into physical reality what you most desire. Personal power is your divine spark and motivation. It gives you peace of mind and keeps you from being a victim.

Items needed:

▶ The personal power pentacle (pictured) en- graved on an iron disk or reproduced on red construction paper.

▶ A small wood box painted red.

▶ A red candle.

▶ A pin.

Using the pin, inscribe your name on the candle. Light the candle and hold it in your left hand and the talisman in your right hand. Chant the following five times with great energy and power:

Glory of Mars, pulsing bright
Bring me power, strength and might.

Place the talisman in the box. Close the lid and set the candle on to of it. Allow the candle to burn completely out. Whenever you feel the need for personal power, take the talisman out of the box, repeat the chant, and carry it with you.

Amulets

The amulet is an object that has been left in its virgin state and is then psychically charged or energized with a specific purpose in mind. Amulets are usually used for pro- tection, as they are passive in their communicative abilities. Only when their barriers have been crossed do they react or retaliate. A good example would be the horseshoe over the door which brings luck to all who cross beneath it; another example is the Udjat Eye, an Egyptian amulet that is sup- posed to bestow invulnerability and eternal fertility.

Udjat Eye

Almost any symbolic object can be turned into an amulet. Special stones, shells with markings, wood carvings, and statues—anything that already exists or is in a natural state can be turned into an amulet simply by forcing your will and dynamic energy into it. Because of its passive nature, and the fact that most of the amulet's power resides in its intrinsic symbolism, a simple blessing or prayer is usually enough to sufficiently charge it.

For example, that lucky horseshoe your grandfather gave you, along with a simple blessing, can be turned into a good luck amulet for all who pass beneath it. Hold the horseshoe in your right hand, and with great emotion, chant the following over it:

> *Iron and speed*
> > *From faithful steed*
> *Grant to all*
> > *what they need.*

Spells for all Occasions

I have been teaching the following spells for years. They are simple to perform and don't require impossible-to-find ingredients. In fact, most of the items used in the spells are readily available in your own home or can be purchased from any mail order house. For those who are so inclined, the recipes for some of the oils and incenses are included as footnotes.

Peaceful Home Spell

Items needed:

▶ One blue candle.

▶ Tranquility oil (equal amounts of ylang-ylang, rose, and lavender oils).

▶ Sandalwood incense.

This spell is especially useful for those who entertain on a business level. There are times when people of varying viewpoints may need to come together in a social atmosphere. To keep things running smoothly, harmoniously, and peacefully use this spell before the party.

One hour before the party take a ritual bath. As you are doing this, begin to visualize the guests as they arrive, seeing in your mind's eye the evening progressing and everyone having a wonderful time. When you finish bathing, anoint your solar plexus with the tranquility oil. This will help you project a positive and harmonious energy level throughout the evening.

Take the blue candle and place it in the room where most of the evening's activities will be held. Now light the incense and carry it throughout the house, saying, as you move from room to room:

Queen of heaven, star of the sea
    Fill this house with love and harmony.
Silver goddess enthroned above
    Let all gather here in peace and love.

Just before the guests arrive, enter the room where you have placed the blue candle and light it. Walk clockwise around that room four times, chanting just as you did in the other rooms. Place the incense next to the candle and wait for your guests.

Spell for Peace and Harmony

Items needed:

▶   Rose quartz.
▶   A mirror.
▶   A pink candle.

Light the pink candle and place it in front of the mirror. Hold the rose quartz in your hands and gaze at the flame reflected in the mirror as you chant the following:

> *O blessed and reflected light*
> *Bring to me peace this night,*
> *Let my mind and heart be free*
> *And filled with love and harmony.*

Look past the flame into the mirror. Try to see which negative elements are affecting you that you want to get rid of. See them being drawn from you into the candle flame and then into the mirror. When you feel the time is right, place the mirror face down. Allow the candle to burn for one hour and then snuff it out. Clean the mirror in salt water and repeat whenever needed.

Money-Drawing Candle Spell

Items needed:

▶   One green candle and holder.
▶   Lavender oil.
▶   A pen or sharp pointed object.

For best results begin this spell on the first night of the waxing moon. Gather the items called for and place them on a small table to serve as an altar. Relax and visualize the amount of money you need. Pick up the candle and inscribe your name near the top of it. In the middle, draw a large dollar sign. At the bottom of the candle write out the exact amount of money you need.

Next, anoint the candle with the lavender oil. Be sure to rub the entire candle with the oil. As you anoint the candle, chant the following.

Money, money come to me
As I will, so it shall be.

Place the candle in the holder and light it. Gaze into the flame of the candle and repeat the chant. Allow the candle to burn for four hours and then extinguish it. Repeat the spell each night until the full moon. On the night of the full moon allow the candle to burn out. You should receive your money before the next new moon.

Money-Drawing Talisman

Items needed:

- ▶ One gold candle.
- ▶ Small square of gold parchment paper.
- ▶ A pen with green ink.

On the night of the new moon, using the pen with green ink, inscribe the talisman pictured here on one side of the parchment paper. On the other side, write exactly what you wish to receive.

Place the gold candle on top of the talisman, light it, and chant the following over the candle:

Gods of prosperity I ask not in greed
But rather for that which I now need.
Fast as the wind swift as the night
Let the money I seek now come into sight.

Allow the candle to burn for one hour. Repeat the spell each night until the candle has completely burned out. On the last night of the spell, after the candle burns out, take the talisman and place it in your purse or wallet. Carry the talisman with you for one full month. At the end of this time, bury the talisman beneath the largest oak tree you can find. Your wish will come true.

Love Attraction Spell

Items needed:

- ▶ One pink candle.
- ▶ A small dish.
- ▶ A heart shaped locket.
- ▶ Basil.
- ▶ Rosemary.
- ▶ Thyme.
- ▶ One thin, green velvet ribbon.
- ▶ Rose oil.

The spell should be performed on a Friday night as close to the full moon as possible. Place all the items called for on a small table that will serve as an altar. Take time to visualize the one you wish to attract. If you have a photograph of the individual you wish to attract, place it on the table as well. Take the candle and inscribe your name on one side and the name of the person you wish to attract on the other side. Connect the two names with intertwining hearts, then anoint the candle with the rose oil as you chant the following seven times:

> *[Insert name] your thoughts are of me*
> *No other face shall you see.*

Set the candle on the dish. Fill the locket with some basil, rosemary, and thyme. Hold the locket close to your heart and say the chant seven more times. Then, placing the locket next to the candle, light it as you chant the following:

With herbs and flame I hold thee tight.
I make thee mine from this night.

When the candle has completely burned out, hang the locket from the green ribbon and give it to the one you desire.

Candle Love Spell

Items needed:

- ▶ A picture of the one you desire.
- ▶ Some of his or her hair.
- ▶ Some of his or her handwriting.
- ▶ A red cloth pouch.
- ▶ A red image candle (pictured here).
- ▶ Rose petals.
- ▶ Rose oil.

On the night of the new moon, gather all of the items needed and place them on your altar. Pick up the image candle and hold it lovingly. Focus on the candle and visualize the one you desire. When you feel the time is ready, anoint the candle with the rose oil as you chant:

Candle of power
    From this hour,
Bring unto me
    The love that I see
That he/she shall requite
    My love from this night

> *Let him/her only see me*
> > *As I now will, So Mote It Be.*

Allow the candle to burn completely out, fill the pouch with the rose petals, the photo, the handwriting, and the hair. Anoint the pouch with the rose oil as you repeat the chant. Whenever you plan to be with this person, be sure to have the pouch with you. Once the relationship is on solid ground, hang the pouch over the entrance to your bedroom for lasting love and happiness.

The Witch's Protection Bottle

Items needed:

One small jar, and enough of the following items to fill the jar:

- ▶ Broken glass.
- ▶ Nails.
- ▶ Thorns.
- ▶ Steel wool.
- ▶ Wormwood.
- ▶ Thistle.
- ▶ Nettles.
- ▶ Vinegar.
- ▶ Salt.
- ▶ Your own urine.
- ▶ One black candle.
- ▶ One red felt marker.

Fill the jar with the items listed above and seal tightly. On the top of the lid, draw a pentacle with the red felt marker. Place the black candle on the lid of the jar and light it. Chant the following over the candle:

Candle of black, and hexes old
   Release the powers that you hold.
Reverse the flow of spells once cast
   Leave pain and sorrow in the past.

Let the candle burn out. Take the jar and bury in the earth close to your home. It will protect you and your family from harm. In most cases it will form a shield of protection for about six months. When the spell begins to weaken, make a new protection bottle.

Goddess Protection Spell

Items needed:

- ▶ Salt.
- ▶ Water.
- ▶ Power oil (equal amounts of petitgrain, clove, and juniper oils).
- ▶ White candle.
- ▶ White parchment paper.
- ▶ A silver-blue pouch.
- ▶ Jasmine incense.
- ▶ Medium clear quartz crystal.

Add nine pinches of salt to the water, saying:

Salt and water now combine
   Protect my heart, protect my mind.
Dark evil forces now fade away
   So that only good shall come my way.

Now sprinkle the mixture of salt water around the area in which you are working. Next, inscribe the protection symbol pictured here on the parchment.

At this point you will want to anoint the candle with the power oil and then place it on the tip of the parchment paper symbol. Light the jasmine incense. Pick up the crystal and pass it through the smoke of the incense as you say the following:

Goddess of the moon I call upon thee,
    For your love and blessings.
Great mistress of all magic protect me
    Give me your power in this my hour of need.

Allow the candle to burn for one hour. Extinguish the candle and place the parchment, vial of oil, and the crystal into the pouch and carry it with you. When you feel negative energies coming at you, rub the oil on your solar plexus and hold the crystal in your power hand (the hand you write with). Repeat the spell once a month on the night of the dark moon for continued protection.

Chapter 13

Resources

"It is certain that if you would have the whole secret of a people, you must enter into the intimacy of their religion."
—Edgar Quinet, French poet (1803-1875)

B y now you should have a good understanding of what Wicca entails as a religious and magickal philosophy. You have probably done some additional reading, created your own sacred space, and are practicing the Craft on a regular basis. If so, you obviously feel comfortable with Wicca, and are at the point where you would like to meet others who share your convictions. The solitary way of life is fine for a while, but sooner or later we all get curious about what our peers are doing. This is especially true with Wicca, as it is very socially oriented. In fact, most of the Pagan rites that have been passed down and are celebrated today were structured for large groups of people.

Once you have decided to journey forth into the world of Paganism, you may find that meeting others of like mind is not as easy as you thought it was going to be. Generally, Wiccans don't hang out signs that read, "Witches live here." For the most part, Wiccans are fairly discreet, and so it can be tricky trying to sneak into their lairs. Moreover, once you finally get past the gatekeeper, you may not like what you see. Don't think for a second that just because someone calls him or herself a Wiccan he or she is an ascended master and knows more than God. Wiccans are just human beings — some are good, some are not so good, and some are better left alone. When it comes to any spiritual discipline it is best to approach with caution until you have all the facts.

Covens and groups that are willing to take on new members usually advertise in Wiccan periodicals, post notices in local bookshops, and are listed on the Internet. Even so, it usually takes time and a good deal of determination to ferret out a reliable teacher or group. The problem is not a lack of quantity, but rather a lack of quality. A lot of public Wiccans act more like hippies than Priests and Priestesses. They also tend to place more importance on the number of people they have in attendance than on the quality of the instruction they offer. This creates an undesirable climate in which to grow and progress spiritually.

However, there is hope. Armed with a few simple guidelines, anyone can procure proper magickal training. The key that will unlock the door of a well-organized group of spiritually minded people is the following common sense evaluator—something everyone should use when approaching a new religious or philosophical organization.

Common Sense Evaluator

The following common sense evaluator is a guide to help you choose the teacher and or group that will be right for you, and help you with the learning process.

1. The very first thing to do is *ask for a printed copy of the basic tenets of the group.* This should include what it believes and how it practices magick and celebrates seasonal rites. Also included should be what the group requires from its membership. If this is not forthcoming, you should seriously question the skills and abilities of the leader and group. Anyone who is running a group, has valid information, and expects to teach and lead others should be able to provide you with a printed copy of his or her group's doctrine—even if it is only one page. So remember, no hard copy, no deal.

2. Ask teachers where and with whom they trained, and then evaluate their responses. Did the teacher provide you with names, dates, and places? Or did he offer you wild tales about being the seventh son of a seventh son, whose grandmother (who is now dead) initiated him in his early teens? No names or dates of training? Look elsewhere.

3. Observe the living conditions of the prospective teacher and group members. Is the teacher able to support him or herself and his or her family? Are the other members of the group clean, drug-free, and responsible? If the teacher and the group are out of control, how can they possibly help you? So, if the place is a mess, run, don't walk, and don't look back.

4. What does the teacher want in exchange for teaching you? Don't buy into the old Wiccan adage that anything spiritual should be free. Some sort of an exchange should take place, whether it is that old demon cash or help around the house. Everything of value has a price—there are no free rides. People who don't ask for compensation for their time and work may have some hidden agenda. This usually manifests itself in power-tripping or cult-like mind control. If the teacher does not state his or her price up front, be wary of what might be expected of you in the future. So, no price, no commitment from you!

5. Ask the teacher for references, and always meet with or interview other members of the group. *The best way to judge the efficacy of any organization is by its membership.* Are the other members responsible, mature adults? Are they friendly, outgoing, and responsive to new people, or are they arrogant, and secretive? Do they speak of spiritual and uplifting ideas or do they hang around and gossip? Do they welcome you in friendship as an equal, or do they expect you to bow in deference? Consider how you feel about the teacher and group before you make a commitment.

6. Be observant. What is the main focus or interest of the teacher and group? Do they spend more time discussing mundane matters than spiritual ideals? Before a Sabbat celebration, do they spend more time discussing what should be on a feast list than on proper ritual procedure? Or, worse yet, do they consider feasting more important than ritual and hurry through the rite so there are more time for fun and games? If the teacher or group are more interested in the chips and dip than in the raising spiritual consciousness, get your own munchies and stay home.

I have selected the following Wiccan/Pagan organizations because they stand for what the Wiccan religion should embrace, encourage, and exhibit. Each organization listed has been in operation for more than 15 years, is legally recognized, and is spiritually oriented. To my knowledge, the groups listed here are not gender biased or single-sex oriented, do not condone the use of drugs, and do not condone promiscuous sexual activity.

To the best of my knowledge, each of the organizations listed meets on a regular basis, is open to newcomers, and stresses structured training by competent teachers. Unfortunately, I cannot make any guarantees regarding the groups, other than Our Lady of Enchantment, as I am its founder and president. I can guarantee that at Our Lady of Enchantment you will receive accurate information and timely service and be welcomed at our open circles.

Note that when writing to any nonprofit organization, it is always a good idea to enclose a large, self-addressed, stamped envelope for a prompt reply and return information.

Organizations

Our Lady of Enchantment Seminary of Wicca
P.O. Box 1366
39 Amherst St.
Nashua, NH 03061
(603) 880-7237
www.wiccaseminary.org
An international, nonprofit religious and educational organization.

Founded in 1978 by the author, Our Lady of Enchantment has a worldwide membership of more than 25,000 students and is the largest legally recognized seminary of Wicca in the United States. The school offers home study courses and personal training in Wicca, magick, and metaphysics. Our Lady of Enchantment is the only Wiccan teaching facility to offer a Wiccan Religious Arts and Science Degree, Priesthood Certification, and legal Ministerial Credentials program. The seminary chapel, gift shop, and library are open daily. Friday night church services, Sabbat celebrations, and full moon ceremonies are open to the public. Our Lady of Enchantment is highly recommended for those seeking a serious, no-nonsense approach to Wicca and the magickal arts.

The Hermit's Grove
9724 132nd Ave NE
Kirkland, WA 98033
(206) 828-4124

The Hermit's Grove is associated with the Rowan Tree Church and is a nonprofit organization. It offers training in a tradition of Wicca that focuses on Wicca as a mystery tradition. Emphasis is on yoga and Tibetan and tantric disciplines. For more information on books, tapes, and study materials, send $2 for a sample copy of the Rowan Tree Church newsletter.

Circle Sanctuary
P.O. Box 219
Mt. Horeb, WI 53572
(608) 924-2216
www.circlesanctuary.org

Circle, since 1974, has been a nonprofit, nature spirituality resource center. Circle serves as a growing network of people in the United States and other countries. Circle emphasizes Wiccan ways, Shamanism, Goddess studies, and nature spirituality. It is headquartered on a 200-acre sacred nature preserve 30 miles west of Madison, Wisconsin. Circle publishes a quarterly magazine, *Circle Network News*, as well as the *Circle Guide to Pagan Groups* and the *Circle Bulletin.* Each year Circle hosts the Pagan Spirit Gathering, a week-long summer festival for Pagans, Wiccans, and their families.

Aquarian Tabernacle Church
P.O. Box 409
Index, WA 98256
(360) 793-1945

The Aquarian Tabernacle Church and center for non-traditional religion is based on English traditional Witchcraft with emphasis on Greco-Roman mysteries. Based in the Pacific Northwest, the Aquarian Tabernacle focuses on sacred stewardship of the land. The church owns and operates a retreat house, which includes an outdoor circle and shrine to the goddess Hecate. The goal of the church is to provide a place for Wiccans and Pagans to meet and celebrate their holy days. It holds monthly worship services called Diana's Bow on the third day after the new moon, and sponsors a spring mystery festival.

Temple of the Eternal Light
928 E. Fifth St.
Brooklyn, NY 11230
(718) 438-4878

The Temple of the Eternal Light is Brooklyn's oldest Kabbalistic Wiccan temple, an eclectic fellowship that approaches Wicca from a magickal point of view. Their home study program and in-house workshops focus on the Thirteen Tools Towards Enlightenment, which incorporate the Kabbalah and ceremonial magick into Wicca. They are nice folks and they meet on a regular basis.

New Wiccan Church (NWC)
P.O. Box 162046
Sacramento, CA 95816

The New Wiccan Church was founded in 1973. It is an international federation of Elders and focuses on British Wiccan traditions. The church is dedicated to the preservation of the initiatory process, in an ethical manner, within the Wiccan religion. NWC publishes *The Red Garters International*. For more information, send a SASE with two first class stamps. They will be happy to send you information regarding membership, networking contacts, and referrals to other groups.

Builders of the Adytum (BOTA)
5101-05 N. Figueroa St.
Los Angeles, CA 90042
(800) 255-0041

Although this is not a Wiccan organization, it is considered to be one of the best schools of Western Mystery Tradition. Established in 1922, BOTA focuses on the Tarot, Kabbalah, alchemy, astrology, and other established metaphysical sciences. It offers a very good correspondence course on the Tarot and its mystical and Kabbalistic associations.

Magickal Products

Unfortunately, Wal-Mart, Macy's, and Sears do not carry pentacle-embroidered capes, consecrated tools, or gift sets containing love-drawing perfume. Consider yourself blessed if you have a well-stocked New Age or Occult store in your town. However, if you are one of the thousands of Wiccans who live in small towns or rural areas, mail order is your best bet. For the most part, the metaphysical supply houses listed here are owned and/or operated by Wiccans and those involved in the magickal arts.

If you are ordering by mail, buy in quantity, as large purchases usually cost less per item than single item orders do. If you order candles, order a full box of each color rather than just one candle each. Order oils in sets, incense in bulk, and charcoal by the box. This will save you time, money, and the frustration of not having what you need when you need it.

Also, there are literally hundreds of sources for magickal products; the following are just a few that I'm familiar with. A good place to begin further research is the Internet, but be careful—there are unscrupulous people out there.

Azure Green/Abyss
P.O. Box 48
Middlefield, MA 01243
(413) 623-2155

All things magickal. Large catalog. Books, candles, ritual items, oils, incense, music, and much more.

Moon Scents and Magical Blends
P.O. Box 180310
Boston, MA 02118
(800) 368-7417

Free catalog. Incense, oil, books, Tarot cards, crystals, jewelry, cauldrons. Nice products, reasonably priced.

White Light Pentacles
P.O. Box 8163
Salem, MA 01971
(800) MASTERY

Traditional New Age, Wiccan, Pagan products. Wholesale and retail. White Light is a distribution network and represents a diverse group of mystical business artisans.

Worldwide Curio House
P.O. Box 17095
Minneapolis, MN 55417

These people have been in business since the Stone Age. If there is something magickal that you cannot find somewhere else, these folks will more than likely have it. They don't call themselves the world's largest for no reason. Their 220-page catalog is $3.

The Excelsior Index Works
1413 Van Dyke Ave.
San Francisco, CA 94124
(800) 423-1125

Exceptional products, including incense, resins, candles, oils, soap, and perfume.

Pyramid Books and New Age Collection
35 Congress St.
Salem, MA 01970

One of the nicest New Age stores around. They are open daily, including weekends. The store carries a wide variety of items, including books on Wicca, Tarot cards, statues, incense, and a very nice selection of jewelry.

Seven Stars
58 JFK St.
Cambridge, MA 02138
(617) 547-1317

If you are having trouble finding a particular book on Wicca, magick, Celtic studies, or any other metaphysical topic, look no further. Seven Stars also carries some of the nicest crystals and gem stones I have seen, as well as Tarot cards, tapes, magazines, and all manner of magickal wonders. You name it, they'll have it (or will get it for you).

Glossary

Every philosophy and religion has its own language. In the following list you will find some of the most frequently used words and terms you will encounter during your studies of Wicca. Take a few moments to look them over. Once you understand the language, the veil of mystery begins to lift and the reasoning behind Wicca begins to make sense.

Altar: A small table usually placed in the center of a circle. The altar is where all obeisance is directed during ritual. The altar reflects the personality of the individual using it. The altar provides the backdrop for ritual, establishes the theme of the magickal work being done, and sets the mood for ceremony.

Amulet: A constructed object, usually made of stone or metal, that is engraved with runes or magickal symbols and used or worn as a charm for protection, love, or good luck.

Astral: Pertaining to the etheric world, the invisible world of spirit, which is close to the mundane world.

Athame: The Witch's double-edged knife, which is used to direct personal power during ritual. It is usually about 9 inches long, has a black handle, and is personally consecrated and charged by the Witch for use in religious and magickal rites. The athame is only used symbolically and never to let blood or cut material objects. It is one of the four sacred tools of the Witch and magician (the others being the pentagram, wand, and chalice).

Blessing: Benediction. The laying on of hands to confer personal power, energy, or good will to a person or material object.

Bolline: A small, white-handled knife used for cutting herbs and inscribing candles for magickal works.

Burning times: The period of time, from roughly the 14th to the 17th centuries, when Witches were persecuted for their beliefs. It is believed that some nine million people were put to death for practicing Witchcraft. It is very doubtful that all of these victims of the Church were actually Witches. Because the Witch hunts were very profitable (those accused were stripped of their property and belongings), it is more likely that greed was the culprit, rather than Witchcraft.

Censer: An incense burner or heatproof container for burning incense and magickal offerings. The censer is usually placed directly on the altar during magickal rites.

Chalice: A Witch's magickal cup. It represents the element of water during magickal rites. It is considered a sacred symbol of the Goddess. The chalice is used for blessing wine and other liquids during ceremonies and ritual acts. It is usually made of silver, or silver lined with gold to emphasize the divine union of opposites. One of the four sacred tools of the Witch and the magician (the others being the athame, the pentagram, and the wand).

Channeling: A New Age term for allowing an outside source or entity to temporarily inhabit one's body and speak through oneself to others.

Charm: To physically act upon an object or person to change its course of action.

Circle: A sphere of magickal energy created by the Witch or magician. The circle is usually marked on the floor physically, and then charged by projecting psychic energy onto its boundary. The circle is a barrier of protection and is used to contain energy raised during magickal rites.

Cleansing: A process by which the practitioner removes negative energies from objects, people, or places. Usually done before ritual or spiritual work.

Cone of power: An invisible, cone-shaped body of psychic energy raised during certain magickal rites and then directed toward an individual or to achieve a definite purpose. Witches will raise the cone of power to protect their land, heal sick friends, or create material abundance.

Conjuration: The act of summoning a spiritual force or energy source.

Consecration: Blessing an object to infuse it with positive energy. Witches and magicians always consecrate magickal tools and all physical objects to be used during magickal operations.

Conscious mind: The logical, thinking, rational part of our consciousness. The place in the brain that manipulates information and processes environmental stimuli received through hearing, seeing, tasting, smelling, and feeling.

Correspondences: Magickal links that work on the principle that like attracts like. For example, a love spell would be enhanced by using correspondences that emphasize the concept of love, such as hearts, flowers, pink candles, and rose quartz.

Coven: A group of Witches, usually led by a High Priestess and High Priest. The coven usually consists of 13 members, who meet on the night of the full moon to work magick and to celebrate the eight seasonal shifts.

Craft: Another term for Witchcraft, magickal practice, and Wiccan spirituality.

Crone: The third aspect of the Triple Goddess, denoting experience, wisdom, and the knowledge that comes with age.

Dedication: The act of committing oneself to the Wiccan God and Goddess and the Wiccan path of spirituality. Dedication, unlike initiation, can be performed by the individual and does not require the presence of an initiated priest or priestess.

Deocil: Clockwise, which is considered to be a positive direction. Most Witches walk deocil when they are within the bounds of their magick circles.

Divination: Fortune-telling using Tarot cards, dice, tea leaves, or Runes to predict the future.

Drawing Down the Moon: A ritual act whereby the High Priestess or Wiccan practitioner draws on the energy of the moon and the Goddess for empowerment.

Elemental: A deliberately formed and controlled thought-form of intelligent energy that is capable of performing menial tasks for its master.

Elements: Air, fire, water, earth. These are considered to be the four building blocks of life and can be used to enhance magickal works. Each element is assigned a direction within the bound of the Witch's magick circle: Earth-North; Air-East; Fire-South; Water-West.

Etheric world: The invisible world of spirit, which is close to the mundane world.

Evocation: The summoning and/or conjuring of a spiritual force. For example, the archangels are evoked to guard and protect the magickal circle, or an elemental might be evoked outside the circle to perform a task for the Witch or magickian.

Familiar: An elemental or a totem animal that has been programmed/trained to be a magickal servant of the Witch. Once the animal has become a familiar it will have a special bond with its master. Spirit forces from the astral plane can also be summoned to act as familiars.

Gaia: A Greek goddess and popular term for the Earth Mother or Mother Earth.

Glamour: The act of casting a magickal spell on another individual using only personal power. Glamour is the art of fascination—making people see, believe, and do things they ordinarily wouldn't.

Green Man: The god who dwells deep within the forest.

Guardian: A higher spiritual force, such as an archangel, who is summoned forth during a ritual to guard and protect the perimeter of the magick circle from any unwanted outside forces or energies.

Incantation: The act of singing, chanting, or speaking formulaic words, phrases, or sounds to raise energy for manipulation during spellcasting and ritual magick.

Initiation: A formal spiritual act that transforms a dedicated individual and his or her view of reality.

Invocation: The act of calling down or summoning a higher spiritual force to add energy to a magickal work. The act of invocation psychically links the individual with the force to aid in the performance of psychic feats.

Linking: The process of using mental identification to communicate with spiritual forces, and/or with appropriate symbols in a magickal operation.

Libation: An offering of wine, water, or other fluid, which is poured on the ground in honor of the God and/or Goddess during or after ritual work.

Macrocosm: The world of reality or the universe that is around us all.

Maiden: The first of three aspects of the Triple Goddess. The maiden denotes youth, beauty, and virtue.

Microcosm: The world of reality that exists within us and everything that exists.

Magick: A system of concepts and methods for using the subtle forces of nature to help the individual alter reality.

Magnetism: Magickal power, life force. The energy projected by the Witch or magician that influences his or her immediate surroundings.

Mighty Ones: The Guardians of the Quadrants, also called Archangels or Divine Emanations.

Mother: The second aspect of the Triple Goddess, denoting fertility, love, nurturing, and the protective qualities of motherhood. The Mother Goddess is the aspect most commonly used in ritual, especially because it corresponds to the full moon.

Mystery Tradition: A religious or magickal order (cult) that meets in secret and requires initiation for admission. The teachings of the order are meant to shed light on the mysteries of immortality and the laws concerning the human mind and its relationship to the body and the cosmos.

New Age: A spiritual trend, dating to the 1960s, that advocates the blending of metaphysical concepts and religious idealism. Key components include incorporating the Goddess into religious philosophy and viewing the earth as sacred.

Offering: A presentation of a gift, such as incense, candles, flowers, food, or drink, to a deity during a ritual. Also messages written on paper and burned in honor of a deity.

Old Ones: The many gods and goddesses worshiped in the Old Religions; gods that predate the Christian era.

Pagan: A follower of nature-based religion. Also a blanket word meaning a heathen, or anyone who is not a Christian, Jew, or Muslim.

Pan: The mischievous god of the woods, often associated with the fun-loving Dionysus. A horned nature god with the torso of a man and the legs and buttocks of a goat.

Pentacle: A talisman used for magickal operations, usually a round disk inscribed with a pentagram, which protects its user and creates a magickal effect.

Pentagram: The five-pointed star, the most powerful symbol of all ceremonial rites. It symbolizes man in control of the four Elements of nature (Air, Fire, Water, Earth). One of the four sacred tools of the Witch and magician (the others being the wand, athame, and chalice). The focal point of the magickal rite, usually placed at the center of the altar.

Philtre: Love potion or herbal aphrodisiac that has a magickal effect on anyone who drinks it.

Poppet: A doll made in a person's likeness. Usually stuffed with herbs, stones, moss, and items belonging to the individual it represents.

Priest: The male leader of a coven or Wiccan church, who has been properly trained and initiated into the Wiccan faith. The priest usually represents the God during ritual.

Priestess: The female leader of a coven or Wiccan church, who has been properly trained and initiated into the Wiccan faith. The priestess represents the Goddess during ritual and is considered to be the spiritual head of the coven or church.

Psychic Awareness: The sensitivity of the body and mind to subtle vibrations that emanate from the astral plane or from other human beings.

Quadrant: One of the four compass points located on the perimeter of a magick circle. Each quadrant marks a station for one of the elemental energies, guardians, or angelic forces that guard and protect the interior of the circle and those within it. Also called watchtower.

Ritual Bath: A bath meant to purify the body and mind before a magick or religious ritual. The practitioner places incense and a candle near the tub, to which salt water has been added. He or she then speaks a personal blessing before entering the water.

Runes: Characters from old Teutonic alphabets, usually etched onto stones or tiles. Used for divination and spiritual guidance.

Sabbat: Wiccan religious festival, celebrated eight times a year. The Sabbats occur on October 31 (Samhain, the Celtic New Year's Eve), December 21 (Yule), February 1 (Imbolc), March 21 (Ostara), April 30 (Beltane), June 21 (Litha), August 1 (Lughnasadh), and September 21 (Mabon).

Scry: To divine the future by gazing into a mirror, crystal ball, or dish filled with water.

Skyclad: Nude.

Solitary: A Witch who practices and works magick alone.

Song-Spell: A lyrical chant or rhythmic song used to captivate and/or control a person, place, or thing for a specified length of time for the benefit of the Witch or magician casting it.

Spell: A period of time during which a person, place, or situation is held in a captive state for the benefit of a person working his or her will.

Talisman: An object that has been made, consecrated, and magickally charged in order to garner protection, attract money and success, or induce love and friendship. A talisman can be made from just about anything, because it is the act of consecration that makes it magickal.

Triple Goddess: A goddess who has three distinct aspects— maiden, mother, and crone—which correspond to the three phases of the moon.

Underworld: The realm that lies just below the surface of the earth. The place where everyone must face the Dweller of the Threshold in the final test of the soul as it progresses from one life to another.

Visualization: Forming mental images to enhance magickal work and spellcrafting. Also, the ability to recreate within the mind an image once seen; total recall.

Wand: The second and most valued of the four major working tools of the Witch (the others being the pentagram, athame, and chalice). It is symbolic of the Air element and is used for directing energy. The wand is phallic in shape and represents the will of the Witch or magician. It is usually the length of the bearer's arm from the tip of the middle finger to the inside of the elbow.

Warlock: A term used by the Catholic Church to denote male Witches. The term is rarely used in Wicca, as both male and female adherents are called Witches or Wiccans.

Webweaving: Networking with other magickal people to exchange information.

Wheel of the Year: Denotes the eight seasonal festivals (Sabbats). The wheel represents the never-ending cycle of birth, life, death, and rebirth. As the seasons change, the wheel turns.

Wicca: A current and more popular name for Witchcraft. A neo-Pagan religion that expresses a reverence for nature and a polytheistic view of deity and that practices simple ceremonies to achieve communion with the natural forces of Mother Earth.

Widdershins: Counterclockwise. A circle of sacred space is usually taken up/removed by walking in a widdershins manner. Opposite of deocil.

Working: A magickal act done to reach a certain state of mind or create a desired effect.

Wortcunning: Herbalist. The term is mostly used by folk healers and Witches who specialize in the secret healing and magickal properties of herbs and plants.

Zodiac: An invisible band in the sky within which the planets are thought to move. The zodiac has 12 places, or houses, in which the planets reside at different times.

Recommended Reading

There is no such thing as a bad book. A book my be poorly written or not to your taste, but that does not make it bad. All books contribute in some way to the perspective and knowledge of a given subject, even if the only information we glean from them is what not to do. When one begins to pursue any magickal or religious philosophy it is always best to consider as many viewpoints as possible before making judgements. The following books offer a variety of opinions and perspectives on Wicca, Pagan mythology, and the magickal arts.

The Wiccan Religion

Budapest, Zsuzsanna E. *The Holy Book of Women's Mysteries.* Piedmont, Calif.: Susan B. Anthony Coven, 1979.

Farrar, Stewart. *What Witches Do.* New York: Coward, McCann and Geoghegan, 1971.

Gardner, Gerald B. *Witchcraft Today.* Secaucus, N.J.: Citadel Press, 1955.

Martello, Leo Louis. *Witchcraft, the Old Religion.* Secaucus, N.J.: Citadel Press, 1975.

Ryall, Rhiannon. *West Country Wicca.* Custer, Wash.: Phoenix Publishing, 1989.

Principles of Wiccan Belief

Farrar, Janet, and Stewart Farrar. *The Life and Times of a Modern Witch.* New York: Piatkus, 1987.

Moorey, Teresa. *Witchcraft, a Beginner's Guide.* North Pomfret, Vt.: Hodder and Stoughton, 1996.

Skelton, Robin. *The Practice of Witchcraft Today.* Secaucus, N.J.: Citadel Press, 1995.

Roots of Wiccan Tradition

Carr-Gomm, Philip. *The Elements of The Druid Tradition.* Boston: Element Books, 1996.

_____. *The Druid Renaissance.* Wellingborough, England: Throsons, 1996.

Mathews, Catlin. *The Elements of The Celtic Tradition.* Boston: Element Books, 1989.

Nichols, Ross. *The Book of Druidry.* Wellingborough, England: Aquarian Press, 1990.

The God and the Goddess

Farrar, Janet, and Stewart Farrar. _The Witch's Goddess_. Custer, Wash.: Phoenix Publishing, 1987.

_____. _The Witch's God_. Custer, Wash.: Phoenix Publishing, 1989.

Pennick, Nigel. _The God Year_. Capall Bann Publishing, 1998.

Robertson-Lawrence, Durdin. _The Year of the Goddess_. Wellingborough, England: Aquarian Press, 1990.

Wiccan Myth and Scripture

Ankarloo, Bengt, and Gustav Henningsen. _Early Modern European Witchcraft_. Clarendon Press,1993.

Bell, Jessie. _The Grimoire of Lady Sheba_. St. Paul: Llewellyn Publications, 1974.

Leland, Charles G. Aradia, _Gospel of the Witches_. Custer, Wash.: Phoenix Publishing, 1990.

Valiente, Doreen. _Witchcraft for Tomorrow_. New York: St. Martin's Press, 1978.

Valiente, Doreen, and Evan Jones. _Witchcraft, A Tradition Renewed_. Custer, Wash.: Phoenix Publishing, 1990.

Principles of Nature

Cunningham, Scott. _Earth, Air, Fire and Water_. St. Paul: Llewellyn Publications, 1991.

Morwyn. _Web of Light_. Atglen, Pa.: Whitford Press, 1993.

Sabrina, Lady. _Reclaiming the Power_. St. Paul: Llewellyn Publications, 1992.

Valiente, Doreen. _Natural Magic_. Custer, Wash.: Phoenix Publishing, 1986.

Sacred Wiccan Symbols

Bowes, Susan. *Life Magic*. New York: Simon and Schuster, 1999.

Cunningham, Scott. *Living Wicca*. St. Paul: Llewellyn Publications, 1993.

Hunter, Jennifer. *21st Century Wicca*. Secaucus, N.J.: Citadel Press, 1997.

Huson, Paul. *Mastering Witchcraft*. New York: Putnam, 1970.

The Wiccan Temple

Crowley, Vivianne. *Wicca, The Old Religion in the New Age*. Wellingborough, England: Aquarian Press, 1989.

Green, Marian. *A Witch Alone*. Wellingborough, England: Aquarian Press, 1991.

Jones, Prudence and Mathews, Catlin. *Voices From the Circle*. Wellingborough, England: Aquarian Press, 1990.

Starhawk. *The Spiral Dance*. New York: Harper and Row, 1979.

Fundamental Rites

Gray, William. *Evoking the Primal Goddess*. St. Paul: Llewellyn Publications, 1989.

————. *Temple Magic*. St. Paul: Llewellyn Publications 1988.

Green, Marion. *Practical Techniques of Modern Magic*. Wellingborough, England: Thoth Publications, 1993.

Seasons of Celebration

Campanelli, Pauline and Dan. *Ancient Ways*. St. Paul: Llewellyn Publications, 1991.

Farrar, Janet, and Stewart Farrar. *Eight Sabbats for Witches*. London: Robert Hale, 1981.

Fitch, Ed. *Magical Rites From the Crystal Well*. St. Paul: Llewellyn Publications, 1984.

Sabrina, Lady. *Cauldron of Transformation*. St. Paul: Llewellyn Publications, 1996.

Wicca and Magick

Bowes, Susan. *Life Magic*. New York: Simon and Schuster, 1999.

Cooper, Phillip. *Basic Magic, a Practical Guide*. York Beach, Maine: Samuel Weiser, 1996.

McArthur, Margaret. *Earth Magic*. Fresh Fields, England: Capall Bann Publishing, 1994.

Sabrina, Lady. *Secrets of Modern Witchcraft Revealed*. Secaucus, N.J.: Citadel Press, 1998.

_____. *Reclaiming the Power*. St. Paul: Llewellyn Publications, 1992.

Watson, Nancy B. *Practical Solitary Magic*. York Beach, Maine: Samuel Weiser, 1996.

Spellcrafting and Natural Magick

de Pulford, Nicola. *The Book of Spells*. London: Quatro, 1998.

Dunwich, Gerina. *Candlelight Spells*. Secaucus, N.J.: Citadel Press, 1988.

Kemp, Gillian. *The Good Spell Book*. Boston: Little Brown, 1998.

Morrison, Sarah Lyddon. *The Modern Witch's Spellbook*. Secaucus, N.J.: Citadel Press, 1971.

Bibliography

Ankarloo, Bengt and Henningsen, Gustav. *Early Modern European Witchcraft*. New York: Clarendon Press, 1993.

Bell, Jessie. *The Grimoire of Lady Sheba*. St. Paul: Llewellyn Publications, 1974.

Bowes, Susan. *Life Magic*. New York: Simon and Schuster, 1999.

Budapest, Zsuzsanna E. *The Holy Book of Women's Mysteries*. Piedmont, Calif.: Susan B. Anthony Coven, 1979.

Campanelli, Pauline, and Dan Campanelli. *Ancient Ways*. St. Paul: Llewellyn Publications, 1991.

Carr-Gomm, Philip. *The Elements of the Druid Tradition*. Boston: Element Books, 1996.

———. *The Druid Renaissance*. Wellingborough, England: Throsons, 1996.

Cooper, Phillip. *Basic Magic, a Practical Guide*. York Beach, Maine: Samuel Weiser, 1996.

Crowley, Vivianne. *Wicca, the Old Religion in the New Age.* Wellingborough, England: Aquarian Press, 1989.

Cunningham, Scott. *Earth, Air, Fire and Water.* St. Paul: Llewellyn Publications, 1991.

_____. *Living Wicca.* St. Paul: Llewellyn Publications, 1993.

de Pulford, Nicola. *The Book of Spells.* London: Quatro, 1998.

Dunwich, Gerina. *Candlelight Spells.* Secaucus, N.J.: Citadel Press, 1988.

Farrar, Janet, and Stewart Farrar. *Eight Sabbats for Witches.* London: Robert Hale, 1981.

_____. *The Life and Times of a Modern Witch.* New York: Piatkus, 1987.

Farrar, Stewart. *What Witches Do.* New York: Coward, McCann and Geoghegan, 1971.

Fitch, Ed. *Magical Rites From the Crystal Well.* St. Paul: Llewellyn Publications, 1984.

_____. *A Grimoire of Shadows.* St. Paul: Llewellyn Publications, 1996.

Gardner, Gerald B. *Witchcraft Today.* Secaucus, N.J.: Citadel Press, 1955.

Gray, William. *Temple Magic.* St. Paul: Llewellyn Publications 1988.

_____. *Evoking the Primal Goddess.* St. Paul: Llewellyn Publications, 1989.

Green, Marian. *A Witch Alone.* Wellingborough, England: Aquarian Press, 1991.

_____. *Practical Techniques of Modern Magic.* Wellingborough, England: Thoth Publications, 1993.

Hunter, Jennifer. *21st Century Wicca.* Secaucus, N.J.: Citadel Press, 1997.

Huson, Paul. *Mastering Witchcraft.* New York: Putnam, 1970.

Jones, Prudence, and Mathews, Catlin. *Voices From the Circle.* Wellingborough, England: Aquarian Press, 1990.

Kemp, Gillian. *The Good Spell Book.* Boston: Little Brown, 1998.

Leland, Charles G. *Aradia, Gospel of the Witches.* Custer, Wash.: Phoenix Publishing, 1990.

Martello, Leo Louis. *Witchcraft, the Old Religion.* Secaucus, N.J.: Citadel Press, 1975.

Mathews, Catlin. *The Elements of the Celtic Tradition.* Boston: Element Books, 1989.

McArthur, Margaret. *Earth Magic.* Fresh Fields, England: Capall Bann Publishing, 1994.

Moorey, Teresa. *Witchcraft, a Beginner's Guide.* North Pomfret, Vt.: Hodder and Stoughton, 1996.

Morrison, Sarah Lyddon. *The Modern Witch's Spellbook.* Secaucus, N.J.: Citadel Press, 1971.

_____.*The Modern Witch's Spellbook II.* Secaucus, N.J.: Citadel Press, 1986.

Morwyn. *Web of Light.* Atglen, Pa.: Whitford Press, 1993.

Nichols, Ross. *The Book of Druidry.* Wellingborough, England: Aquarian Press, 1990.

Ryall, Rhiannon. *West Country Wicca.* Custer, Wash.: Phoenix Publishing, 1989.

Sabrina, Lady. *Reclaiming the Power.* St. Paul: Llewellyn Publications, 1992.

_____.*Cauldron of Transformation.* St. Paul: Llewellyn Publications, 1996.

_____. *Secrets of Modern Witchcraft Revealed.* Secaucus, N.J.: Citadel Press, 1998.

Skelton, Robin. *The Practice of Witchcraft Today.* Secaucus, N.J.: Citadel Press, 1995.

Starhawk. *The Spiral Dance.* New York: Harper and Row, 1979.

Valiente, Doreen. *Witchcraft for Tomorrow.* New York: St. Martin's Press, 1978.

_____. *Natural Magic.* Custer, Wash.: Phoenix Publishing, 1986.

Valiente, Doreen, and Evan Jones. *Witchcraft, a Tradition Renewed.* Custer, Wash.: Phoenix Publishing, 1990.

Watson, Nancy B. *Practical Solitary Magic.* York Beach, Maine: Samuel Weiser, 1996.

Index

A

Air, Element of, 69-70
Alexandrian Wicca, 16-17
All Hallows' Eve, 117-122
Altar, the, 84-85, 117
Amulets, 172-173
Apollo, 46
Arch-Druid, 33
Aridia, 19
Astral Projection, 158-160
Athame, 79, 82
Autumnal Equinox, 146-152

B

Bards/Bardd, 33
Beltane, 134-135
    ceremony for, 136-138
Brigantia, 126-129
Brigid, 52-53

C

Candle love spell, 178-179
Cartomancy, 161
Casting a magick spell,
    166-169
Celtic clergy, 33
Celtic Druids, the, 31-39
    basic beliefs and
        practices, 34
Cernunnos, 46
Cerridwen, 53
Chalice, 80, 82
Charge of the Goddess,
    62-63
Common sense evaluator,
    185-187
Correspondences
    Air, 70
    Earth, 75
    Fire, 71
    for days of the week, 168

Water, 73
Council of American
   Witches, 22
Council principles, 22-25
Coven laws, 27-29
Covens, defined, 10
Craft, the, defined, 9-10
Creating sacred space, 85-86
Creative Visualization,
   156-158
Crystallomancy, 161-162

Deity, 41-55
Demeter, 53
Descent of the Goddess,
   60-62
Devotional Witchcraft, 15
Diana, 53
Dianic Wicca, 17
Dionysus, 46
Divination, 160-161
Drawing Down the
   Moon, 65-66
Druid/Derwydd, 33

Earth, Element of, 74-76
Eclectic Wicca, 17

Elemental Tool Symbolism
   chart, 81
English Witchcraft Act, 14
Enochian, 16

Faunus, 46
Fire, Element of, 70-72
Five Forces of Influence,
   the, 35
Fortune, Dion, 14
Four Elements, the, 36, 67-76
Full moon, 101
   celebrating the, 103-114
   names, 102-103
   rituals
      for solitary practice,
         104-107
      for three or more,
         108-114
Functional Witchcraft, 15
Fundamental Rites, 91-114

Gardner, Gerald, 14-16
Gardnerian Wicca, 15-18
God months, 19
God, 9, 42-43
God/dess, honoring the, 116
Goddess, 9, 15-17, 48

months, 19
protection spell, 180-181
worship, 14
Great Days, defined, 115-117
Great Rite, the, 16
Guardians, calling in
the, 87-89

Harvest God, the, 45-46
Hecate, 53
Hereditary Wicca, 18
High Magick's Aid, 16
Horned God, the, 16, 44-45

Imbolg, 126-127
ceremony for, 127-129
Intention, 92, 95-96
Invocation, 92-93
of the God, 94-95
of the Goddess, 93-94
Isis, 53-54

Kabbalah, 16

Lammas, 142-146
Law of Three, 33
Logical Order of the
Triad, 33
Love attraction spell,
177-178
Lugh, 46
Lughnasadh, 142-143
ceremony for, 144-146

Mabon, 146-148
ceremony for, 148-152
Magick, defined, 153
and Wicca, 153-163
four cornerstones
of, 155-156
principles of, 154-156
Magickal
process, 156-163
products, 191-193
Masonic ritual and
Wicca, 14
Masons, 16
Mathers, MacGregor, 169
May Eve, 134-138
McFarland, Morgan, 17
*Meaning of Witchcraft,
The,* 16

Midsummer, 138-139
    ceremony for, 140-142
Money-drawing candle
    spell, 175-176
Money-drawing talisman,
    176-177
Moon Goddess, the, 48-49
Morrigan, the, 54
Mother Goddess, the, 50-51
Myth of Esus and Tarvos,
    58-60

Natural magick and
    spellcrafting, 165-181
Nemeton, the, 38-39
Nichols, Ross, 14

Organizations, 188-191
Osiris, 47
Ostara, 130
    ceremony for, 130-134
Ovates/Ovydd, 33

Pagan gods, 42
Pagan rites, 14

Palmistry, 162-16
Peace and harmony spell,
    175
Peaceful home spell, 174
Pentacle, 80-81
Personal power talisman,
    171-172
Principles of magick, 154-156
Principles of Wiccan
    belief, 21-29

Ra, 47
Rhea, 54
Rite of Union, 96-99
Rituals, 92
Roberts, Mark, 17

Sabbats, defined, 115-117
Sacred circle, 84
    casting the, 87
Sacred space,
    closing the, 89-90
    creation of, 92
Sacred Symbol, 37-38
Salt and water,
    consecration of, 86-87

Samhain, 117-119
  ceremony for, 119-122
Sanders, Alex, 16
Seasons of celebration, 115-152
Seasons of the God/dess, 54-55
Shamanic customs, 14
Sol, 47
Solitary Rite of Union, 100-101
Spell
  candle love, 178-179
  for peaceful home, 174
  for peace and harmony, 175
  Goddess protection, 180-181
  love attraction, 177-178
  money-drawing candle, 175-175
  money-drawing talisman, 176-177
  witch's protection bottle, 179-180
Spell, defined, 165
Spellcasting, associations and correspondences, 170
Spellcrafting and natural magick, 165-181
Spells, casting, 166-169
Spiral of Abred, 34-35

Spiritual knowledge, 10
Spring Equinox, 130-134
Strega Wicca, 18-19
Summer Solstice, 138-142
Sun God, the, 43
Symbols, sacred Wiccan, 77-82

Talismans, 169-172
Tammuz, 47
Traditional Wicca, 18
Traditions of Wicca, 15
Transcendent Three, the, 35
Triple Goddess, the, 51-52

Udjat Eye, 172-173

Valiente, Doreen, 14

Wand, 78-79
Water, Element of, 72-74
Wheel of the Year, 36-37

Wicca,
  and Magick, 153-163
  defined, 9-10
  origins of, 13-14
Wiccan
  belief, principles of, 21-29
  myth and scripture, 57-66
  religion, 10, 13-19
  roots, 31-39
  temple, the, 83-90
Wiccan Rede, 15, 25-26
Winter Solstice, 122-126
Witch's Mystical Triangle,
  157-158

Witch's protection bottle,
  179-180
Witchcraft Today, 16
Witchcraft, 10, 13-14
  defined, 9-10
Witches' Chant, the, 64-65

Yule, 122-123
  ceremony for, 124-126

About the Author

Lady Sabrina is an initiated priestess of the Wiccan religion and the founder of Our Lady of Enchantment, the largest federally recognized Wiccan seminary in the United States. During the last 20 years, Lady Sabrina has taught more than 25,000 students worldwide how to develop their personal power through Witchcraft and magick. She has appeared on major television talk shows and is the author of many books, including *Secrets of Modern Witchcraft Revealed, Reclaiming the Power,* and *The Witch's Master Grimoire.* Sabrina lives in New Hampshire with her three dogs, two cats, and assorted fish. She enjoys crafts, gardening, antiquing, and old horror movies.